Jean Shaw

HERB GARDENING

CHANCELLOR
PRESS

Acknowledgements

This book has been compiled with material previously published by Reed International Books.

Additional text by Suzy Powling, Jenny Plucknett, Richard Rosenfeld, Meg Sanders and Stella Vayne.
Illustrations by Jim Robins and Rod Sutterby.
Symbols by Coryn Dickman.

The publishers would like to thank the following organizations and individuals for their kind permission to reproduce the photographs in this book:

A-Z Collection 71; Boys Syndication 49/Jacqui Hurst 31; Eric Crichton 30, 38, 40, 44, 51, 60, 66, 67, 69; Brian Furner 37; Garden Picture Library 64/Derek Fell 33; Andrew Lawson 45; Tania Midgley 68; Photos Horticultural 56; Reed International Books Ltd 57, 65/Michael Boys 28, 32, 34, 42, 46, 48/W.F. Davidson 36, 43/Melvin Grey 21/Jerry Harpur 41/Neil Holmes 29, 35, 50, 53, 55, 59, 61, 70/George Wright 63; Harry Smith Collection 47, 52, 54, 58, 62;Peter Stiles 39

First published in Great Britain in 1995
by Chancellor Press, an imprint of Reed Consumer Books Limited
Michelin House, 81 Fulham Road, London SW3 6RB
and Auckland, Melbourne, Singapore and Toronto

ISBN 1 85152 628 5

A catalogue record for this book is available from the British Library.

Produced by Mandarin Offset, Hong Kong
Printed in Hong Kong

Contents

INTRODUCTION

When you grow herbs, you are growing history. Many of the herbs we use commonly today were grown hundreds, even thousands, of years ago. The earliest surviving written accounts of using herbs date back to 2000BC in Babylon, but herbal medicine was used well before then. Herbs have been subject to so much less intensive breeding than, say, ornamental plants that many are unchanged from the times when they provided the only source of medicine, flavouring, scent and cosmetics available.

The role of herbs in our lives has certainly changed but as plants they still easily earn their place in the garden even if we have other ways of fulfilling some of the needs they once answered. Now that growing herbs is no longer, literally, a matter of life and death the decorative qualities of herbs, as well as their more utilitarian characteristics, can be taken into account when planning and planting, and a herb garden can be every bit as attractive and just as much fun to develop as a strictly ornamental one.

VARIETY AND CHOICE Although herbs are often considered together as a single group of plants, they are extremely varied. Ranging from half-hardy annuals to woody shrubs, they take in just about every category of plant there is as well as offering a huge variety of size and shape from tiny creeping thyme to towering angelica. Although this means you have to know how to treat each one individually, it also means that herbs considered as a group can be very adaptable to garden situations. There are a good many herbs that thrive on shallow, well-drained soil and in full sun, but equally there are herbs that will give of their best in moist, cool soil and in partial shade. In general, however, herbs are tough, good-tempered plants and will perform quite satisfactorily even in conditions that are far from ideal.

The choice of what to plant and where to plant it depends, in the case of herbs, not just upon your garden situation but also on the use you intend to make of the herbs you grow. For herbs are not only a decorative addition to your overall garden design – they are functional too. Herbs required for regular culinary use are best situated near to your kitchen so they are readily available in all weathers. If scent is your priority, place the herbs near a sitting area or along a path where they can be fully appreciated, and preferably with sun and shelter, too, so that the scented oils will hang in the air and surround you with their fragrance. For cosmetic and medicinal use you will probably need fairly large quantities of specific herbs, so grow them with the same attention as you would give to vegetables – in sunny, sheltered conditions, with optimal soil and suitable feeding – to get the best results.

Of course, any herb that is going to be consumed should be positioned as far away from car fumes as possible, and grown without routine spraying for pests and diseases. Most herbs are naturally healthy plants and grow very well without the use of pesticides, but herbs grown among other plants may suffer from spray drift. Thorough washing will help, but always have regard to the manufacturers' instructions when using garden chemicals.

A GROWING INTEREST Once you develop an interest in herbs, it is difficult to resist adding new species and varieties to your collection. Again, the wide variety of herb types means that you can use a range of propagation techniques to increase the specimens you already have or to grow new ones. Some herbs are embarrassingly easy to grow from seed – once you have borage and fennel in your garden, for example, you have them for life and not always just where you want them. Others can simply be divided, and yet others must be coaxed from semi-ripe cuttings. If you have a knack for making parsley germinate or for striking rosemary cuttings, your plantlets can be exchanged with herb-loving friends so that you can extend not only the quantity but the variety of herbs you grow cheaply and easily. But even for those inexperienced at propagation, it is worth experimenting with herbs, like basil or parsley, that are used fresh in large quantities – the gain in convenience of being able to crop them just as you need is tremendous.

Fortunately, if even these simple techniques elude you, herbs are cheap to buy in pots and most of the shrubby types, with a little nurturing, can be planted out once they have grown on. Herbs for sale in supermarkets, however, are grown in a way that makes them particularly short-lived. They should simply be kept on a light windowsill and used fairly rapidly in cooking.

HERBS IN THE GARDEN Since herbs are so varied in habit there are many that combine very well with other plants in your garden, so there is no need to group them all together in a specific herb garden. In a large garden this might indeed be an attractive option and there are plenty of examples of formally laid out herb or physic gardens to inspire you. Confined within low box hedges, planted to form sometimes complex geometric patterns, they have an old-world charm of their own, but would probably look out of place in small, modern gardens. Fortunately, herbs can also be interspersed in mixed borders with plants grown solely for decorative purposes, and they hold their own very well both in terms of vigour and appearance. Not all are decorative enough – few gardeners would plant horseradish in a prominent position – but there are plenty to choose from that earn their place in the ornamental border through the appeal of their flowers, foliage and form.

HERBS IN CONTAINERS Another characteristic of many herbs that makes them perfect for gardeners with limited space is their suitability for growing in containers. Even without a garden, and in the most unpromising situations, you can enjoy growing and using herbs provided you choose wisely and treat them with reasonable consideration. Container growing is suitable for many different aspects and widely varying scales of cultivation – from chives and parsley in pots on the windowsill to impressive standard bay trees flanking the front door – but the same principles apply for growing healthy plants anywhere: good preparation is always worthwhile.

Soil Preparation

To grow herbs successfully it is important to care for the soil and to raise healthy plants that can resist pests and diseases.

ACID OR ALKALINE SOILS How well plants grow also depends on how acid or alkaline the soil is. In a slightly acid soil, ideal for vegetables, most nutrients dissolve slowly and can be taken up by the roots. If the soil is too acid nutrients can be washed away altogether or lie in toxic quantities in the soil water while vital phosphorus becomes unavailable to plants. Earthworms, so important for improving the structure of the soil, will move out of a very acid soil. If the soil is alkaline, trace elements become insoluble and cannot be taken up by plants.

Use one of the widely available testing kits to check the pH of your soil. A neutral soil has a pH of 7; anything below that is acid, anything above is alkaline. Most vegetables grow best on a soil with a pH value of 6-6.5. If your soil is too acid, adding lime will help. The quantity needed will depend on your soil type: clay will take more than a sandy soil. Be cautious when using lime, as over-liming can be very harmful, and only apply lime every three to four years. Adding calcified seaweed will also make the soil less acid. To increase the acidity of an alkaline soil add large quantities of rotted organic matter.

IMPROVING YOUR SOIL In the wild a plant grows, taking nutrients from the soil, then dies back and, aided by worms, insects and bacteria, the rotted plant returns those nutrients to the soil so that they can be used again by other plants. In cultivation, and especially in the vegetable and fruit garden, this balanced cycle is broken because we harvest the plants and tidy up the garden by removing dead material. We therefore need to replace the naturally rotted organic matter each year by digging in manure or garden compost.

Apart from supplying food for the growing plants, digging in organic matter improves the soil's structure. Worms, insects and beneficial bacteria are attracted by the supply of food and multiply. Worms and insects improve the aeration of the soil by burrowing; in addition, worms provide fertilizer in the form of worm casts. Some bacteria help in the process of decay while others fix nitrogen from the air into the soil.

Bulky organic matter also helps to turn clay particles into larger crumbs and holds these crumbs apart so that drainage will be improved. It also coats the particles of sand so that the water drains less easily.

ANIMAL MANURE The manure provided by herbivores is an excellent soil conditioner. Contact local stables for supplies of horse manure, which is better if it is based on straw bedding rather than wood shavings. Cow manure is not as readily available as it used to be as a result of current cattle-rearing methods. If you live in the country look for a local farmer who turns out his cattle in the summer in the hope that he has supplies to spare at the end of the winter. Sheep manure is high in nutrients so if you live near a sheep farm ask the farmer if you can collect it off the fields. Pig manure is also high in nutrients and chicken manure is very rich.

Do not use fresh animal manure on the garden. It needs to rot down completely first as in the fresh state it can burn plant leaves and stems, and the decomposing straw it contains will use up nitrogen in the soil. Leave it to decay for at least two to three months, longer if possible. If you can only get small quantities, add it to the compost heap where it will speed up decomposition. Larger quantities should be stacked and covered, especially through winter to protect the heap from bad weather. If you are worried about hormones fed to cattle or chickens, or pesticides that may remain in the straw, it is wiser to leave the manure for at least a year before using it.

GREEN MANURE Green manure is a quick growing crop that is dug back into the soil, while still young and green, to improve the soil's structure. If you have an empty bed, especially if your soil is light and free draining, it is better to sow a green manure like mustard, winter tare or red clover than leave the soil bare when rain can destroy the structure, nutrients drain away and weeds start to grow. Although the growing plants remove some nutrients, when dug back they provide more. As an alternative to digging the plants back into the soil they can be chopped off and left on the surface to be incorporated when they have decayed.

GARDEN COMPOST A very good source of bulky organic material, free to us all, is household and garden vegetable waste. This again needs to decompose before it can be added to the soil. A compost container not only looks tidy but it speeds up decomposition by keeping the material warm. You can simply pile the material in a heap but it will take longer to rot down.

Waste material shrinks considerably when decomposing and the house and garden waste from one family results in a depressingly small heap, too small to provide all the bulk that a vegetable garden will need. You can increase the quantity by collecting waste from local vegetable shops or market stalls.

TIPS ON CREATING GOOD COMPOST Make the size of the container as large as you can: 1sq m/3sq ft is the minimum practical size. If your garden is very small, purpose-built compost bins are available.

Use good insulating materials for the container to help maintain the heat in the heap. Line the base of the container with a 15-cm/6-in layer of coarse material like straw or tough stalks or use wire mesh laid over widely spaced bricks to allow air to circulate.

Add about 20cm/8in of fresh mixed material to the container at any one time. The easiest way of doing this is to place waste materials first into a black dustbin liner, mix up, then add the contents when full. By adding a mixture of materials, the heap remains well aerated and doesn't pack down.

Include any fresh or cooked plant or vegetable waste from

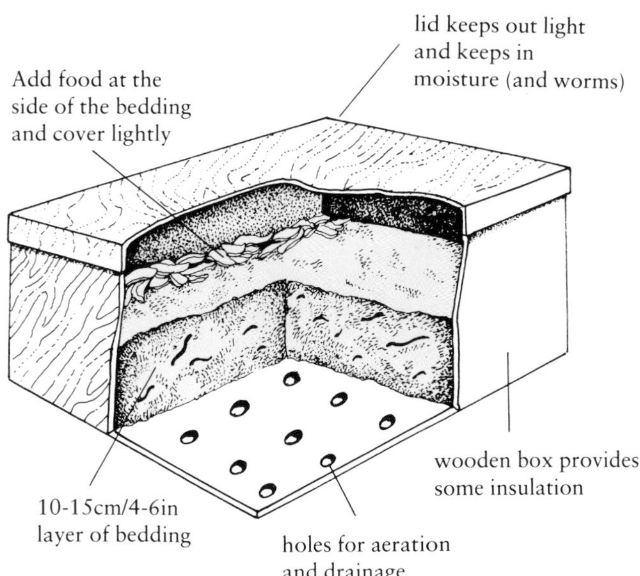

Worm box *Moist compost, shredded newspaper or leaves make up the bedding in the base. The worms are fed with vegetable and kitchen waste.*

the house or garden, including lawn mowings. Slightly woody stems will need shredding or chopping.

Do not include animal waste which may attract vermin, woody material such as hedge clippings or rose prunings which will take a long time to break down, any diseased or infected plant material, weeds that have gone to seed or roots of perennial weeds like ground elder, couch grass or creeping buttercup.

The bacteria which act to decompose the material put on the heap need air, moisture and nitrogen. The water is mainly obtained from the leaves put on the heap but you should water dry materials like straw before adding them. Including animal manure in the heap will help to provide nitrogen, as will seaweed or seaweed extract or a proprietary compost activator. Adding lime helps to neutralize the natural acidity. The bacteria prefer a less acid environment so this will also help to speed up decomposition.

Compost needs to be covered to keep the heat in and to prevent the material becoming too wet. An old piece of carpet or black plastic is suitable. In summer a heap should be ready for use in about three months, in winter it will take more like nine months.

MAKING A COMPOST BIN If you have the room make the compost bin with three separate compartments, one in which to put fresh waste material, one which has been filled up then left to rot down and one of compost ready for use. The sections can be made from timber planks or breeze blocks on three sides of the square with removable wooden boards on the fourth side so that the compost is easy to get at.

WORM COMPOST Worm casts are very rich in nutrients in a form that is readily available to plants, so the compost produced in a worm box is closer to a fertilizer than a compost. The worms used are brandlings which are used by fishermen, and are available from fishing shops. In the base of the box (see illustration on page 13), place a layer of moist compost, shredded newspaper or leaves. Feed the worms with a mixture of chopped-up vegetable and kitchen waste; include some protein which they also need. Animal manure is also suitable. Do not add huge quantities of material, no more than a 7.5cm/3in layer per week. Add some calcified seaweed because the worms do not like acid conditions. The worms will work best between 13-25C/55-77F and will die in freezing weather so cover the box with old carpet to insulate it. Some of the compost can be removed after 2 months.

DIGGING In most years it is only necessary to dig the soil, or fork it, to the depth of a spade blade. However, every three to four years it is a good idea to dig more deeply. This stops a compressed layer forming below the cultivated section which will impede drainage and it allows compost or manure to be included at a deeper level. The deeper cultivated soil encourages plant roots to go downwards, drawing nutrients from a greater depth, and this means that they are also more able to withstand drought. Plants can also be grown closer together.

Double digging is done in a similar way to single digging (see illustrations overleaf) except that the soil at the bottom of the trench is loosened to a further blade's depth with a fork. A good layer of manure or compost is put into the bottom of the trench, then the soil from the second trench is spread over the manure in the first and soil and compost are forked to mix them. The last trench is filled with the soil from the first.

Heavy soils are usually dug in autumn. The surface is left rough so that frost will help to break up the heavy clods. The surface is forked lightly in the spring before sowing or planting. The soil in a narrow bed can be formed into a long ridge and covered in manure. This helps drainage and still allows the weather to break up the soil. With light soils it is better to cover the surface with compost or manure through the winter but leave any digging until the spring.

Once the soil has been dug it is important to keep off it. The structure of the soil is easily destroyed so it is wise to keep beds to a size that allows you to attend to growing plants without going on to the soil. Lay a plank on the surface if you have to walk on it.

WEEDING Perennial weeds with creeping root systems, like ground elder, or deep tap roots, like dandelions, need to be dug out and burned. Include even the smallest piece of root.

Annual weeds will gradually decrease over the years if you make sure that you never allow them to flower or seed and remove them as soon as you see them, or even better hoe to remove them before they reach the light. Mulching will help considerably by cutting off the light from emerging weeds but this cannot be done until vegetable seedlings are through.

WATERING In dry weather it is better to water less often, but thoroughly, than frequently and lightly. Light watering simply encourages roots to grow near to the surface and these will immediately suffer in dry weather, whereas deeper roots have a reserve to draw on. It takes time for water to sink through the soil. Check by pushing a finger into the ground:

How to Dig Correctly

First, chop at right angles to the trench,marking out only a small bite at a time.

Holding the spade vertically and, placing one foot on the tread, cut down parallel to the trench.

Slipping one hand down to the base of the handle turn the clod over into the previous trench.

it can look very wet on the top and feel bone dry only a short way below the surface. It is at a deeper level that roots need water.

FEEDING PLANTS Fertilizers are used to supply extra nutrients to growing plants when needed. They are applied in two ways, either before planting or sowing as a base dressing, which is raked or forked into the soil, or as a top dressing, which is sprinkled around the growing plants, or, if in liquid form, applied with a watering can around the base of a plant.

Plants need the following nutrients plus some trace elements to grow.

NITROGEN – N This is important for leaf growth.
PHOSPHATE – P This is necessary for root growth and for young plants and new shoots.
POTASH – K This aids the production of flowers and fruit and keeps plants healthy.

To provide supplies of one or all of these nutrients you can use a chemical or organic fertilizer.

CHEMICAL FERTILIZERS These can contain one major nutrient or are a compound, a balance of all three. They are easy to use, produce quick results and promote high yields but organic growers would argue that flavour suffers and plants are more prone to pests and diseases. Furthermore, artificial fertilizers do not put anything back into the soil itself for the next generation of plants.

ORGANIC FERTILIZERS These are usually gentler in action and so there is no danger of giving plants too much, which can occur with a chemical fertilizer.

GROWING HERBS

CREATING A HERB GARDEN Even if you have only a balcony or backyard, or no outdoor space at all, it is still possible to grow a range of herbs in pots. A small area of, preferably sunny, free space will give you the chance to plan a decoratively-shaped herb garden. Alternatively, the plants can be intermingled with flowers, or grown in a bed on their own close to the kitchen.

DESIGNING A DECORATIVE HERB GARDEN First, design the garden on paper. In a square plot you could copy the old cartwheel shape, using treated timber fence posts in place of spokes and a bird bath or sun dial as the centre point. Or use the same shape but divide off the sections with 'spokes' of shingle, grass or brick paths. Paths can also be used to divide up a rectangle and form beds of triangles, diamonds and hexagon shapes to break up the space. On a long, narrow plot use an old wooden ladder, or timber laid in a ladder shape, to act as a decorative plant divider.

Leave some of the paving slabs out when designing a patio and plant low-growing evergreen herbs such as thyme and winter savory in the spaces. Group a number of decorative pots together and group tall herbs, such as lovage, angelica and fennel, in the larger pots at the back. Place smaller plants in the front. A line of lavender, rue or rosemary plants can form a low dividing hedge between patio and grass.

AMONG THE FLOWERS Herbs mingle well with flowers and fruit, encouraging pollinating insects with their wonderful scents. Group different varieties of one herb together. Thyme, sage and mint all come in a range of leaf colours and patterns. Create a border for a herbaceous bed with parsley, thyme, chives, marjoram or salad burnet. Tall herbs like angelica, lovage, fennel, southernwood and evening primrose will add decorative leaf shapes towards the back of a bed and shelter smaller, more delicate flowers.

KITCHEN HERB BED If the area outside your kitchen door is sunny then this is an ideal spot for a culinary herb bed and some pots. It also means that you don't have to make a damp dash for a fistful of parsley in wet weather. A bed about 1 by 3 metres/3.3 by 10ft is ideal. If it is wider, you will need stepping stones to help you care for and harvest plants at the back without treading on the soil.

LIMITED SPACE HERB GARDEN Hanging baskets can be used for herbs that will trail decoratively, like marjoram, thyme, nasturtiums, tarragon and chamomile. Boxes will take the more upright varieties, or plant a number of window boxes, each containing plants for specific uses, one of culinary herbs, one of herbs for making herbal teas, one for those herbs used in beauty preparations.

A box on a bedroom or living-room windowsill could be used for strongly scented herbs so that on sunny days herbal fragrances fill the room.

Rampant herbs like lemon balm and mint are more easily controlled if you grow them in a container, so plant them in pots, even if you intend growing them in a window box; then sink them into the soil with the rims about 2cm/¾in above soil level. Delicate herbs like basil and lemon verbena are best grown in pots so that they can be brought indoors in the autumn for protection from frost.

INDOOR HERB GARDEN Herbs grown or brought indoors will be available for picking later into the winter than those grown outdoors. However, plants raised indoors cannot be expected to grow to the same extent as outdoor plants. Therefore, more plants are needed to provide a comparable harvest.

Indoor-grown herbs need ventilation but not draughts, humidity, a moderate temperature of about 15C/60F, good light, and sunshine. The kitchen, unfortunately, is not the ideal spot to grow herbs as temperatures tend to fluctuate too much and unless the ventilation is good, the plants' leaf pores can become clogged with grease and dust. Consider growing them in hanging baskets, pots, or a window box in a sunny window. If you are short of space just grow the herbs necessary for a bouquet garni in a decorative pot: parsley, thyme and bay.

CHOOSING THE HERBS TO GROW The herbs you decide to grow will depend on your own requirements. Some herbs provide a wide range of uses and are found in all categories. Given below are some of the most widely used herbs under each of four main headings.

FOR CULINARY PURPOSES Start off with a limited

number of the herbs you use most, then gradually extend the range, experimenting with species new to you. The ten most popular culinary herbs are: parsley, thyme, bay, rosemary, chives, tarragon, mint, sage, marjoram and fennel.

MEDICINAL HERB GARDEN Most herbs are in one way or another good for healing. Ten starter herbs to treat some minor ailments are: peppermint for indigestion and as a pick-me-up, chamomile for indigestion, fennel for flatulence, lemon balm for insomnia and relaxation, bergamot for insomnia, hyssop for coughs and colds, and parsley to stimulate digestion and as a diuretic herb – it gives gentle stimulation to the kidneys. Rosemary helps to stimulate circulation and when steeped in oil is a help for rheumatism, if gently rubbed into the affected part; sage is an expectorant while thyme stimulates appetite and aids digestion.

COSMETIC HERB GARDEN Many herbs can be included in shampoos, conditioners, moisturizers, cleansers and for bathtime relaxation. Some aid a healthy skin, others hair, eyes, hands, feet or nails. Elder cleanses, softens and whitens skin and is helpful for freckles and wrinkles. It also makes a soothing eyebath. Chamomile, *Matricaria chamomilla,* is good for skin, hair and eyes. Lavender can be used for skin and feet, rosemary for hair and skin, dill for eyes and nails, sage for skin and fennel for cleansing.

FOR SCENT Close to a window plant lemon thyme, lemon verbena, lemon geranium, pineapple mint and sweet marjoram. To attract butterflies and bees include borage, hyssop and thyme.

CULTIVATION Most herbs are a delight to grow. They take little from the soil, while giving off scent, taste and colour. Most also have an in-built rejection of pests and disease.

In fact even if you are totally committed to fertilizers and pesticides, this is an area of the garden where it is important to use organic principles, a start to becoming a committed organic gardener perhaps. As many herbs are used uncooked, and taste to some extent is lost through washing, it has to be better to refrain from including the chemicals in their cultivation.

CHOOSING A POSITION Choose a sunny corner if possible as most herbs thrive in the sun. Those suitable for more shady areas are angelica, fennel, mint, tansy, sorrel and

Herbs grow well in pots and hanging baskets. A good thick moss is required for lining the baskets to prevent loss of moisture.

bergamot. Some protection from wind, such as walls or fences, is valuable.

DRAINAGE A well-drained site is important for almost all herbs so that air can circulate around the plant roots. Soggy soil is airless and cold. The aim is to have a soil that does not dry out too quickly but has good drainage. If you are unsure if your drainage is adequate you can do a simple test. Dig a hole twice the depth of your spade blade and leave it open for a few days. If water collects in the hole over this time it shows that the drainage is poor. The surest way to improve poor drainage is to install pipes laid on gravel and leading to a soakaway point. In practice this is expensive and troublesome for the amateur gardener. An easier, but still laborious, alternative is to dig narrow trenches and partly fill them with large stones before replacing the soil. In most domestic gardens it is enough to dig the ground over to twice the spade's depth and incorporate as much bulky organic matter as you can get.

SOIL AND NUTRIENTS Most herbs grow best in a slightly alkaline soil. The soil should be well dug before planting and organic matter, animal manure, green manure, or garden compost included. For more information see pages 11-14. A healthy organic garden includes a good worm population to aerate the soil, improve drainage and convert materials into plant food. When making your own compost, include any herb refuse as this is specially valuable to the compost heap. Add organic matter in autumn and mulch with a thin layer of compost in spring. This should be all the feeding necessary.

INCREASING HERBS Annual herbs can be sown in warm weather on the spot where they will grow or started indoors to give earlier crops. Recycle seeds for use in the next season but buy new every two to three years.

Perennials can be increased by layering: mint, marjoram, lemon balm, southernwood and sage are all suitable for this method of propagation. During the growing season stem cuttings can be taken from healthy plants (as described and illustrated step by step overleaf). In autumn or early spring when plants are dormant many can be dug up and divided (see illustration on page 26).

HARVESTING Small quantities of most herbs can be cut for use fresh throughout the growing season. However, if you wish to preserve them then the best time to pick is when the volatile oil content is greatest. The time of day and the time in the plant's cycle are the two points to consider. Most herbs should be cut in the morning when the dew has dried naturally but before the sun is fully on the plant. In bright sun the volatile oils, which carry flavour and value, diminish.

If it is the leaves you require, the ideal time to pick is between the formation of flower buds and the opening of the flowers, when the oil content is highest. If you wish to harvest flowers these should be picked when fully open, and in prime condition. Seeds are gathered when the flowerheads begin to turn brown. To check if seeds are ripe, tap a head lightly; the seeds will fall when ready. Cut the heads, including a length of stem, and hang upside down in a dry airy shed. You can either encase the head in a paper bag so that the seeds fall into it or place a basket lined with paper or a cotton cloth below to catch the seeds. Place seeds in airtight containers in the dark to retain the full flavour.

PRESERVING Herbs can be dried in three ways. The traditional method is to tie them in small bunches so that air can circulate freely around the herbage, then hang them upside down in a warm, airy spot for a few days.

The modern alternative is to dry them in the dark on racks. Stretch muslin over a frame (alternatively use 3 metal drying racks) and place leaves, still on the stem, on these. Spread out well in a single layer. Place another layer of muslin on top to keep off any dust and place the trays in a warm, dark place - either an airing cupboard, or the plate-warming drawer of an oven, with the door left ajar ideally. Check if they are ready after 24 hours. When dry, the leaves will feel dry and be brittle to the touch. They should still be green; if they have turned brown the heat was too intense and the flavour will have been lost. Store immediately after cooling in glass jars, preferably dark in colour but otherwise in the dark, to retain strength. Flowerheads should be dried in the same way. Remove as much stalk as possible and handle very carefully as they disintegrate easily.

It is also possible to dry herbs in a microwave. Lay out on a double layer of kitchen paper, place a second double layer of paper over the top and, using the lowest setting on the microwave, check every minute, turning the sandwich each time. They should be ready in 2-4 minutes.

Some herbs, in particular basil, parsley, chives, chervil, dill and tarragon, are difficult to dry successfully and are better frozen. Chop parsley and chives and store in small bags or add a little water and freeze in ice cube containers. Chervil, fennel, dill and tarragon can be left as small sprays and packed in plastic bags. Basil leaves are best picked off the stem and stored in the freezer in small bags.

Taking Cuttings of Shrubby Herbs

Take a cutting of a semi-ripened shoot in summer. Neaten off the end by making a sharp diagonal cut with a knife.

Carefully strip the leaves off the lower end of the cutting to leave sufficient stem bare to insert into the compost. Do this gently with your hands.

Wet the bottom end of the cutting with water and dip it in a pot of hormone rooting powder, which will encourage roots to grow.

Fill trays or pots with seed compost or half-sand, half-peat mixture. Using a matchstick, make holes in the compost and insert the cuttings.

Firm in the cuttings carefully with your fingertips, then gently water them; it is best to use a fine rose on a watering can to do this.

Cover the cuttings with a clear polythene bag, keeping the polythene off the leaves. Place on a warm windowsill but keep out of direct sunlight.

Lifting and Dividing Chives

Lift mature or overcrowded clumps out of the ground, using a garden fork.

Divide the chives into smaller clumps by prising the roots apart with your hands or a small fork.

Plant out the new divisions, without delay, in the desired position. Make sure that the chives are well watered.

A-Z of Herbs

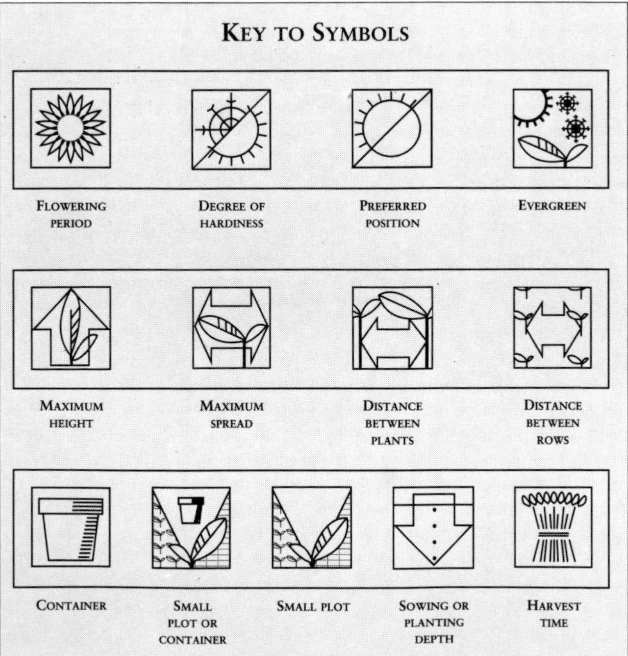

Key to Symbols
Flowering period
Degree of hardiness
Preferred position
Evergreen
Maximum height
Maximum spread
Distance between plants
Distance between rows
Container
Small plot or container
Small plot
Sowing or planting depth
Harvest time

ANGELICA

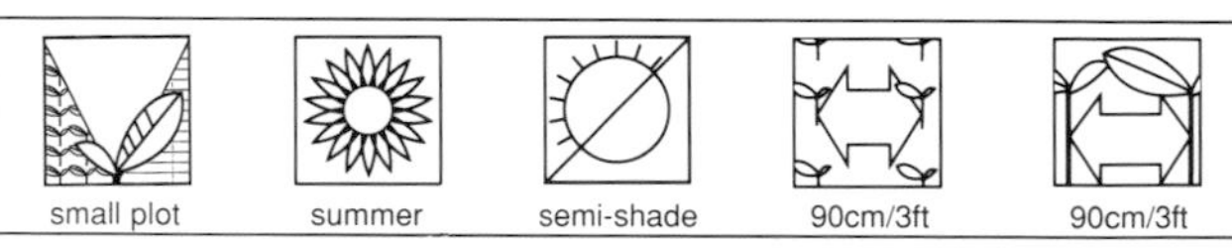

The edible parts of angelica are the hollow stem, which is candied for use in cakes and puddings, and the roots and leaves, which may be cooked with acidic fruits like rhubarb for a milder flavour. As a medicinal herb, it was used to make a soothing tea. Its decorative qualities are many, and at up to 2.4m/8ft high it easily merits a place at the back of a border where it will act as a windbreak for less sturdy plants. The mop-head white flowers which appear in early summer are coveted by flower arrangers – like all hollow-stemmed plants they will last a long time if the plants are up-ended and filled with water (hold your thumb over the stem end until you have placed them in the vase). All parts of the plant are pleasantly aromatic.

PROPAGATION AND GROWING Sow seed in late summer in the open ground and thin the seedlings to 15cm/6in in the first instance, thinning again if necessary. Alternatively start with a young plant and set out in spring. Although it is a biennial, angelica will keep going for several seasons if flowerheads are not allowed to form. The plants will take three or four years to reach maturity; if they flower the plants will self-seed very freely.

VARIETIES There are no varieties of the species, *Angelica archangelica (above)*.

POSSIBLE PROBLEMS Generally trouble-free.

ANTHEMIS

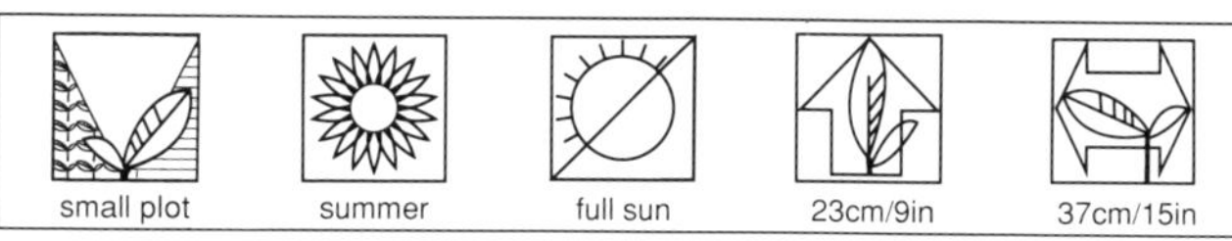

Anthemis nobilis is the name for the perennial plant more commonly known as chamomile. A member of the daisy family – *Compositae* – all species bear small daisy-like flowers of white, cream, yellow or orange. The exception is the flowerless variety 'Treneague', which is the one most suitable for an aromatic lawn or path. The apple-banana scent of the foliage drifts up when the plants are walked upon, and is most fragrant on summer evenings.

PROPAGATION AND GROWING For a lawn, set out young plants in any ordinary well-drained soil in spring 15cm/6in apart each way. A light mowing may be necessary once or twice during the summer. Flowering species for ground cover or window-boxes should be planted out from autumn to spring. Every autumn after flowering, cut down the old stems. To propagate, divide and replant the roots in the autumn or spring.

VARIETIES *A. cupaniana*: white flowers with bright yellow centres, grey-green fern-like foliage; *A. nobilis*: mat-forming, white flowers, mid-green foliage; *A. nobilis* 'Florae Plena' *(above)*, the double-flowered variety has the strongest scent. *A. n.* 'Treneague': flowerless variety.

POSSIBLE PROBLEMS Generally trouble-free.

ARTEMISIA

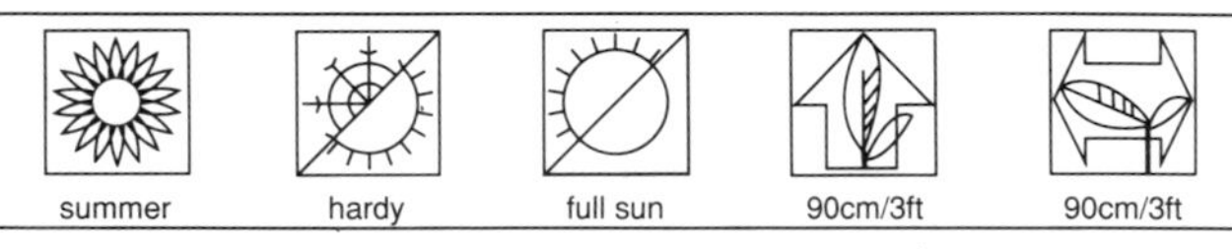

Artemisia abrotanum (above), is a favourite of old cottage gardens, where it acquired its endearing common names of lad's love or old man. Also known as southernwood, this shrubby plant bears spherical, parchment yellow flowers in panicles over the summer; but it is grown for its silky, grey-green fine foliage, with an aroma both sweet and refreshing.

PROPAGATION AND GROWING Plant in spring on any ordinary garden soil with an open texture. Remove the flower stems when they fade. The plant dies down in winter. Pruning should not be necessary, unless to remove straggly growth in spring. Propagate from semi-hardwood cuttings taken in late summer.

VARIETIES *A. arborescens* or common wormwood is a slightly less hardy species which will, nevertheless, reach 1.8m/6ft against a sunny wall. The silvery foliage releases its fragrance when bruised.

POSSIBLE PROBLEMS Aphids; rust.

BASIL

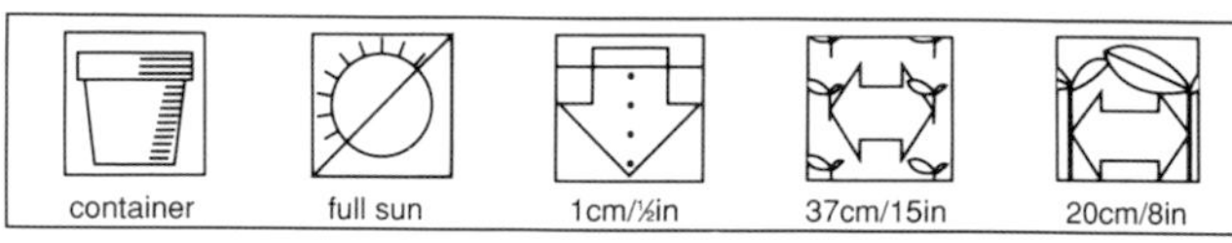

Basil is a half-hardy native of tropical zones which is best treated as an annual in cooler climates. It is a member of the mint family, highly esteemed by good cooks, and is best used fresh. Basil is an essential ingredient of the Genoese sauce *pesto* and the *soupe au pistou* of Provence. Tomato salad is not the same without it. The best culinary species is *Ocimum basilicum* or sweet basil *(above)* which reaches 60cm/24in or more with a spread of 30cm/12in.

PROPAGATION AND GROWING Sow seed indoors in spring. After a hardening-off period plant out in early summer in a warm, sheltered position in light, well-drained soil. Water when dry, but never saturate the soil. Remove the flowerheads as soon as they form.

VARIETIES O. *minimum* or bush basil: a dwarf form at 15-30cm/6-12in high, useful for container cultivation and with a good flavour.

POSSIBLE PROBLEMS Generally trouble-free in suitable conditions.

BAY

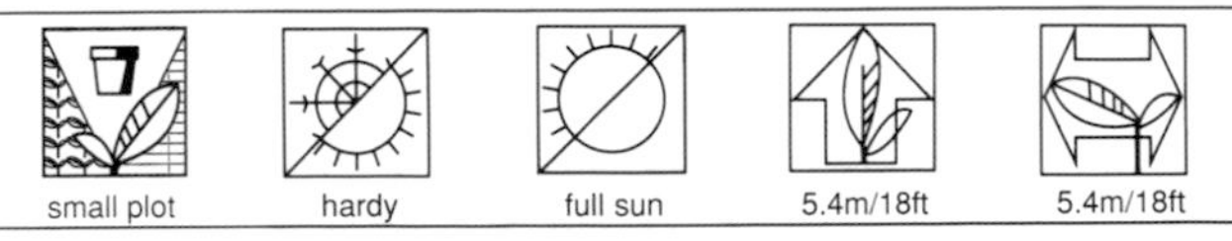

The leaves of the sweet bay, *Laurus nobilis (above)*, were used in ancient times to fashion a crowning wreath for heroes; in medieval times they were included among strewing herbs to sweeten and disinfect the house. In gardens of classical design immaculately clipped bay trees are an essential feature. As a culinary herb too, bay is indispensable, whether in a bouquet garni, added to the poaching liquid for fish, in stews and soups or even in rice pudding. An evergreen, its leaves have as much flavour in winter as in the height of summer, a rare quality among herbs.

PROPAGATION AND GROWING Set out young plants in spring on any type of soil. A sunny, sheltered spot is preferable – leaves are easily damaged by sharp winds. Most trees will reach about 3.6m/12ft in maturity if left alone. Specimens grown in tubs (of about 45cm/18in in diameter) should be pruned to shape during the summer. Propagate from cuttings taken in late summer, or by layering low-growing shoots.

VARIETIES There are no named varieties.

POSSIBLE PROBLEMS Scale insects.

BERGAMOT

		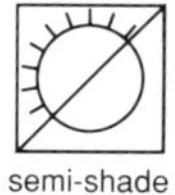	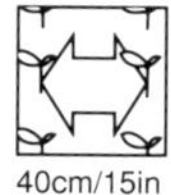	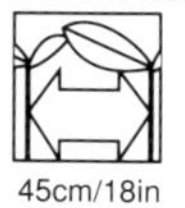
Small plot	summer	semi-shade	40cm/15in	45cm/18in

Bergamot, or *Monarda didyma (above)*, belongs to the *Labiatae* family, which also includes the mints, lavender, rosemary and thyme. It distinguishes itself in such famous company by its spectacularly colourful flowers of red, pink, white or purple. The dried leaves are used in pot-pourri, but the whole plant is impregnated with a delightful fragrance. Its attraction for bees gives it the popular name bee balm; in the USA it is called Oswego tea, after the American Indians who used it for a relaxing aromatic brew.

PROPAGATION AND GROWING Because bergamot is shallow rooting it must be kept moist at all times. Start with young plants and set them out in clumps in spring or autumn – single specimens look lost in a border. Mulch with moisture-retaining material such as peat or leaf mould and provide short stakes. These hardy herbaceous perennials reach 60cm-1m/2-3ft but die down in winter. For a more colourful display, do not allow the plant to flower in the first season. To propagate, divide the clumps in spring.

VARIETIES 'Cambridge Scarlet'; 'Croftway Pink'; 'Snow Maiden'; 'Blue Stocking'.

POSSIBLE PROBLEMS Generally trouble-free.

BORAGE

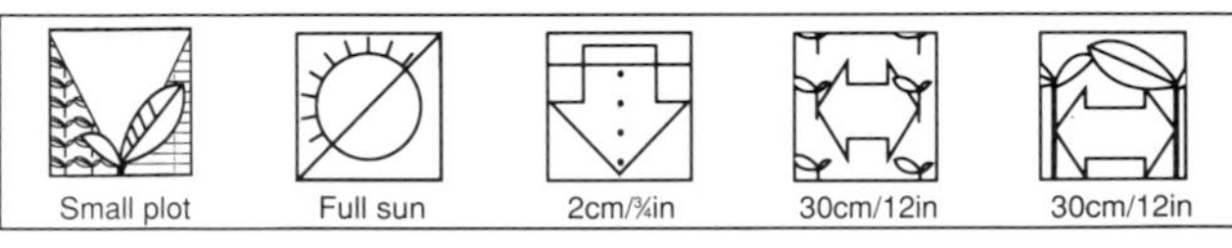

Like many plants with deep blue flowers, *Borago officinalis (above)* – a member of the forget-me-not family – is very attractive to bees. The flowers are seen to best advantage when grown in clumps,and as they may reach 90cm/3ft some form of support may be necessary for the stems. Borage earns a place in the herb garden because of its leaves, which have a refreshing cucumber-like taste. They can be used in salads, and are ideal to decorate a cool summer drink.

PROPAGATION AND GROWING Sow seeds in spring where they are to flower in any ordinary well-drained, garden soil. Successive sowing will ensure a supply of leaves through the summer. The leaves should be ready for use within 6-8 weeks and should always be used perfectly fresh. Propagation of this hardy annual is easy – borage self-seeds very freely and may become a nuisance if not kept in check.

VARIETIES There are no named varieties.

POSSIBLE PROBLEMS Generally trouble-free.

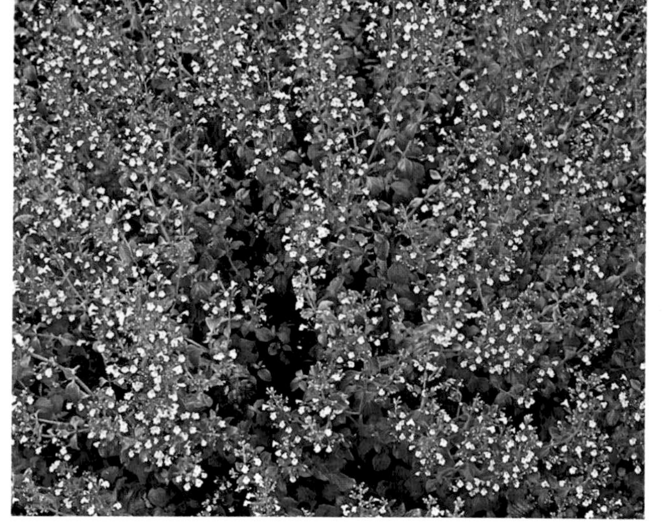

CALAMINTHA

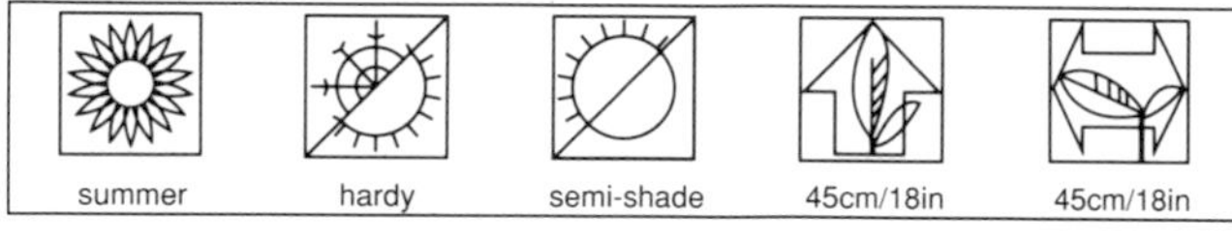

The minty aroma of *Calamintha grandiflora (above)*, is released by bruising the foliage. A cloud of tiny pink flowers covers the plant in summer, making it suitable for cottage gardens or for a 'wild' corner. According to some old herbals, a handful of crushed calamint leaves could be used to relieve cramp.

PROPAGATION AND GROWING This perennial is happiest in full sun on well-drained soil, but will do well in partial shade as long as the soil is not too moist. Plant in spring. The plant self-seeds, but can be divided in autumn if wished.

VARIETIES C. *alpina*: 10cm/4in high, light green leaves and mauve flowers on trailing stems, good for rock gardens.

POSSIBLE PROBLEMS Generally trouble-free.

CARAWAY

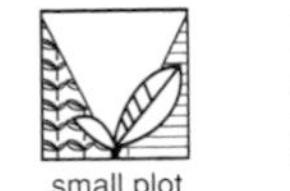
small plot

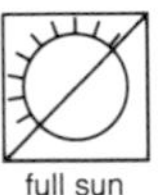
full sun

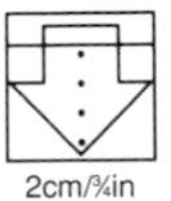
2cm/¾in

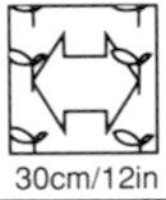
30cm/12in

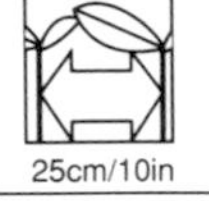
25cm/10in

The graceful flowerheads of caraway, borne on top of 60cm/24in stems, identify it as a member of the parsley family, *Umbelliferae*. It is grown chiefly for its 'seeds' (actually fruits), which when ripe are added to cakes and bread or cream cheese. The leaves have something of their spicy aroma and are good freshly chopped and scattered over vegetable soups. The essential oil contained in the seeds is good for the digestion, and is released simply by chewing them. It is used in the liqueur Kummel. Caraway has been cultivated in Europe for centuries for medicinal purposes.

PROPAGATION AND GROWING Sow seed in early summer in light well-drained soil in a sunny position. Germination is swift. As biennials the plants reach maturity in the second year; in severe winters protect the seedlings with a mulch. Remove the seedheads before they burst open and dry them indoors. Dig up the plants at the end of the second year (sow every year for a continuous supply). The roots are edible – treat as carrots.

VARIETIES There are no varieties of the species, *Carum carvi (above)*.

POSSIBLE PROBLEMS Generally trouble-free.

CHERVIL

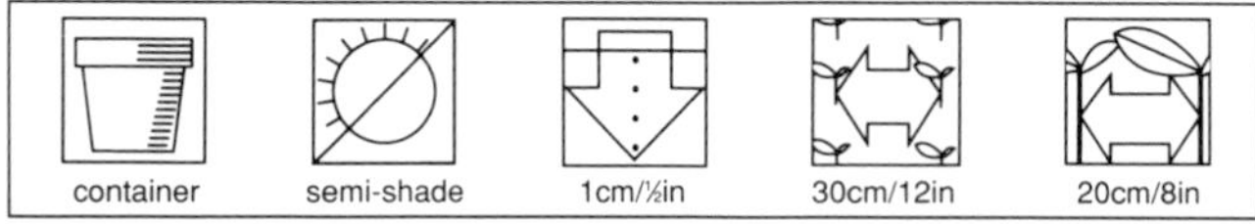

Chervil is related to parsley and is not dissimilar in flavour, though more delicate in appearance. Its botanical name is *Anthriscus cerefolium (above)*. Generous quantities are needed for cooking, particularly for delicious chervil soup. Like parsley, chervil is best used fresh, not dried, and makes a good accompaniment to vegetables and dishes based on eggs or cheese.

PROPAGATION AND GROWING A hardy annual, chervil is quick to germinate, and with successive sowing you can be sure of supplies all year. From early spring to late summer sow seed in any type of well-drained soil. Leaves can be picked once the plants have reached 10cm/4in. The mature height is about 45cm/18in. Protect the plants with cloches during the winter, or grow in pots and bring indoors.

VARIETIES There are no varieties of the species.

POSSIBLE PROBLEMS Generally trouble-free.

CHIVES

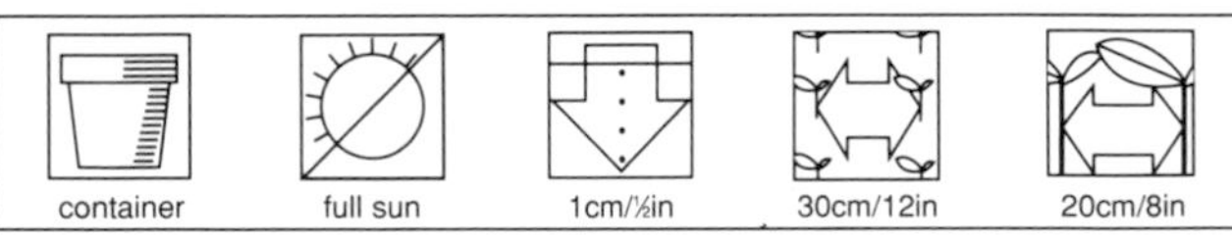

Chives are one of the most important culinary herbs, with a mild onion flavour. The chopped leaves can be used to garnish soups, salads and cooked vegetables, in omelettes or mixed with cream cheese. The narrow grass-like leaves grow in clumps up to 37cm/15in high. Pink pompon-shaped flowers appear in summer, pretty enough to qualify chives to be used as edging plants in a cottage garden (and, with luck, keep greenfly off the roses). For the best flavour, however, flower-heads should not be allowed to form. There is no reason why you should not grow some chives in the herb garden or in a tub for the kitchen and others for decorative purposes in the garden proper, allowing only the latter to come into flower.

PROPAGATION AND GROWING Chives may be raised from seed sown in shallow drills in spring and transplanted in early summer; or you can start with young plants and set them out in light, moisture-retentive soil. Water well in dry periods. Every few years, in the autumn, divide the clump into several sets and replant them in fresh soil. Chives do well in window-boxes or small pots, which can be kept indoors for a winter supply.

VARIETIES There are no varieties of the species, *Allium schoenoprasum (above)*.

POSSIBLE PROBLEMS Leaf-tips turn brown if the plant becomes dry.

CORIANDER

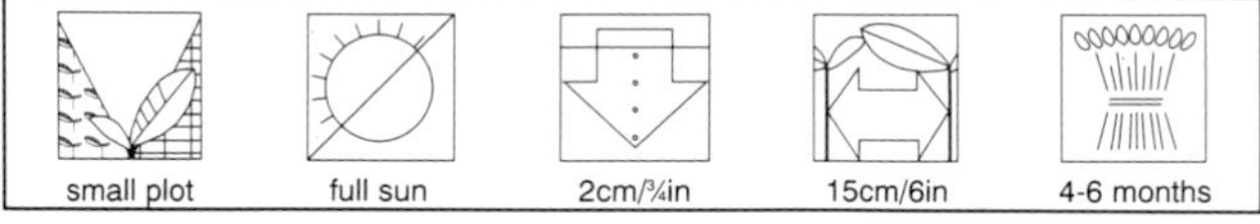

Coriander is a hardy annual grown both for its seeds, which have a warmly aromatic flavour, and for its lower, scallop-shaped leaves which are invaluable in eastern cuisine, being used rather like parsley. The flavour is much sharper than that of the seeds and rather lemony.

GROWING Sow in a sunny, sheltered position in light, rich soil during early spring. If the seeds are to ripen, the longest possible growing season is needed, so don't delay sowing until any later in the year. The leaves are at their most aromatic just before the small white flowers open. The small round beige seeds can be gathered in the autumn and either stored whole in an airtight container or ground down to a fine powder. The sooner it is used the better. After several months it begins to smell like cardboard.

POSSIBLE PROBLEMS Generally trouble-free.

USES Add seeds to meat or chicken curries for flavour and the bright green leaf colour. Fresh leaves can be added to salads.

COSTMARY

	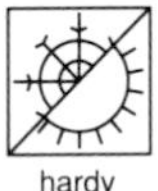	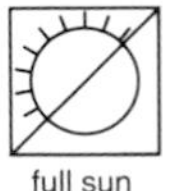	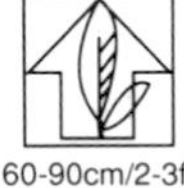	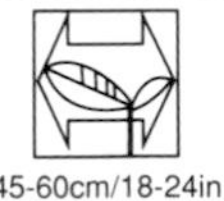
autumn	hardy	full sun	60-90cm/2-3ft	45-60cm/18-24in

Also known as alecost or herb st mary, costmary was one of the strewing herbs used to refresh Tudor households with its deeply penetrating scent of camphor. Correctly listed as *Chrysanthemum balsamita (above)*, it is a herbaceous perennial sometimes found as *Balsamita major* or *B. vulgaris*, and should not be confused with balsam (*Impatiens balsamina*, a half-hardy annual with large scarlet flowers). The daisy-like flowers of costmary are tiny, which may explain its rarity today. But the little blooms are numerous, the large elliptical leaves intensely aromatic, and at 90cm/3ft high costmary well deserves a place in a fragrant border.

PROPAGATION AND GROWING Plant from autumn to spring in fertile, well-drained soil. A sunny position is best, but some shade is tolerated. It is best to cut back after flowering. To propagate, divide established plants in autumn or spring.

VARIETIES There are no other varieties

POSSIBLE PROBLEMS Earwigs.

DILL

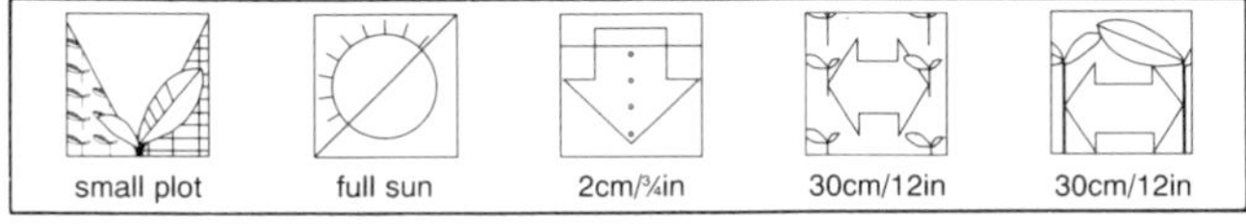

A decorative herb, dill looks at its best when a number of plants are clumped together in the herb bed. The needle-like leaves, and tiny yellow flowers from early to late summer, make it difficult to distinguish from fennel. Both the aromatic leaves and seeds are used.

GROWING Sow seed where it is to grow, in a well-drained soil and a sunny position. Cover the seed with a light sprinkling of soil. Make successive sowings from mid spring to early summer for a continuous supply of leaves. Stake the plant if the site is windy. Cut off the flowers of some of the plants as they appear so you can pick and use the leaves. Other plants can be left to go to seed. As soon as the flower-heads are brown, the seeds are ripe. The whole plant should then be cut down and the seed drying completed indoors.

HARVESTING Leaves can be used from six weeks after germination.

POSSIBLE PROBLEMS Watch for aphids.

USES Dill leaves make a particularly good sauce to go with fish. Add chopped leaves to green and raw vegetables, especially cucumber, and sprinkle over grilled lamb chops. Use whole or ground dill seed in lamb stews, herb butters, bean soups and in pickled baby cucumbers. Dill seed tea is good for the digestion and will also help you to sleep.

FENNEL

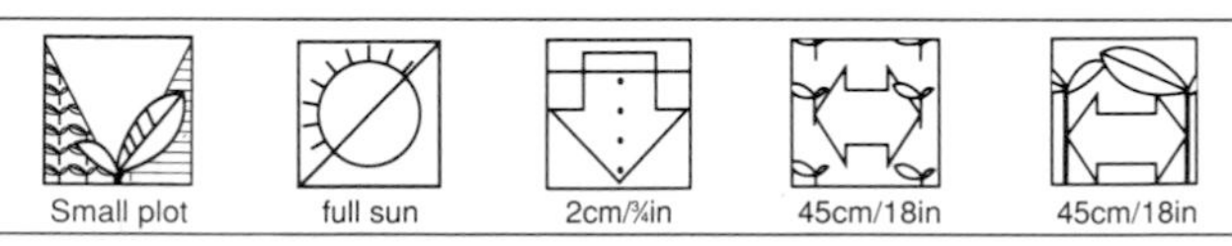

Another member of the *Umbelliferae* family, fennel – *Foeniculum vulgare (above)* – is both highly decorative, with feathery bluish-green leaves, and very useful in the kitchen. The anise-like flavour is even stronger in the dried seeds than in the leaves. Like its close relative, dill, fennel is an aid to digestion. The leaves are best used to accompany fish vegetables and salads, the seeds in bread or soups. At 2.1m/7ft high this herbaceous perennial makes a stately addition to the border; it has been said that after a shower of rain a big bush of fennel looks like blue smoke.

PROPAGATION AND GROWING Sow seed in late spring, in well-drained, rich soil. If seed is not required, remove the flower-stems as they appear. Self-sown seedlings will appear freely if plants are allowed to flower; if not, propagate by dividing the parent plants every three years or so. The seeds are ready to harvest when they are grey-green and have hardened. Cut off the whole flowerhead and dry slowly indoors.

VARIETIES True green and bronze forms are available, much sought-after by flower arrangers. *F.v. dulce* is the vegetable Florence fennel, with similar foliage but grown for its swollen bulb-like stems.

POSSIBLE PROBLEMS Generally trouble-free.

FEVERFEW

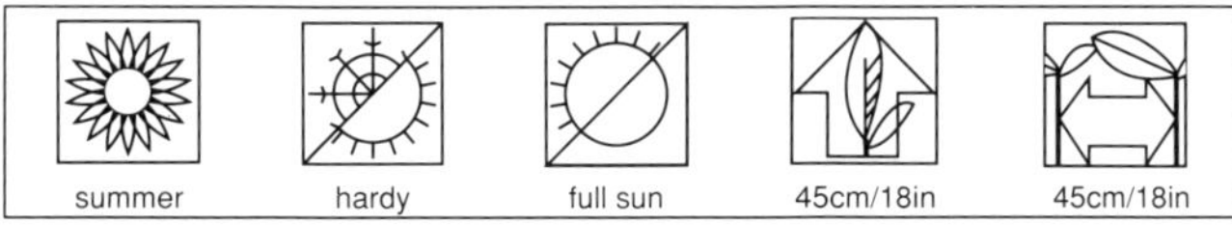

Like chamomile, to which it is closely related, feverfew *Chrysanthemum parthenium (above)*, is a member of the daisy family. It is a short-lived perennial usually grown as an annual which bears white or yellow flowers. The light green, deeply cut leaves have a sharp aroma. As a wild flower, feverfew rejoices in the common name flirtwort. Disappointingly, however, old herbals recommend it not as a love potion, but as a mild laxative.

PROPAGATION AND GROWING Sow seed in spring in fertile, well-drained soil. A sunny site is best, but some shade will be tolerated. Seed germinates easily, so it is best to raise new plants each year.

VARIETIES 'Aureum': green-gold foliage, single white flowers; 'White Bonnet': double, white flowers. Dwarf varieties ideal for pots and window-boxes are sometimes listed under *Matricaria eximia*; they include 'Golden Star', 20cm/8in high, with clusters of round yellow flowers and 'Snowball', 30cm/12in, with neat round white flowers.

POSSIBLE PROBLEMS Earwigs; aphids, cutworms.

GARLIC

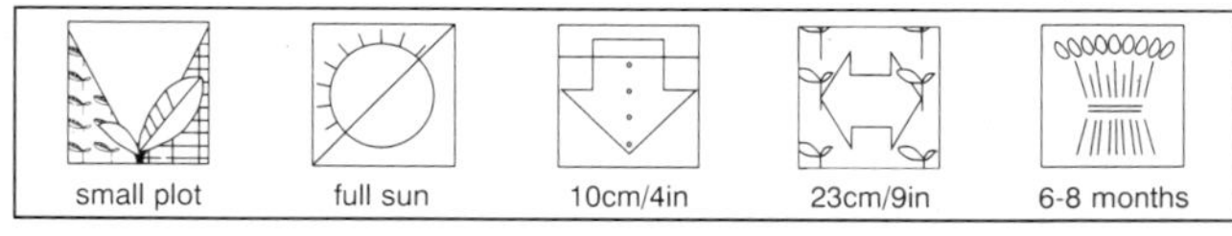

Essential for anyone who cares about food. Pluck your own bulbs fresh and zingy from the soil.

GROWING For a handful of large succulent garlic, plant outside in light, well drained soil in late autumn or late winter, provided the ground is not frozen. First, buy the largest, healthiest garlic available and detach the cloves. Plant out point uppermost, 10cm/4in deep and water in well. As soon as the flower heads start to develop, pinch them out to divert extra nourishment to the bulbs which are swelling just beneath the soil surface. You can expect to harvest in mid- to late summer, and any bulbs that you do not use immediately can be dried in the sun then stored in a dry, cool and frost-free place. Select good-sized cloves for replanting for the following year.

HARVESTING When the onion-like green leaves turn brown and start to die down, lift and use. Handle with care since they easily bruise.

POSSIBLE PROBLEMS Heavy wet clay soils are highly unsuitable.

USES Roasted individually; in stews and curries; pasta sauces.

GERANIUM (SCENTED-LEAVED)

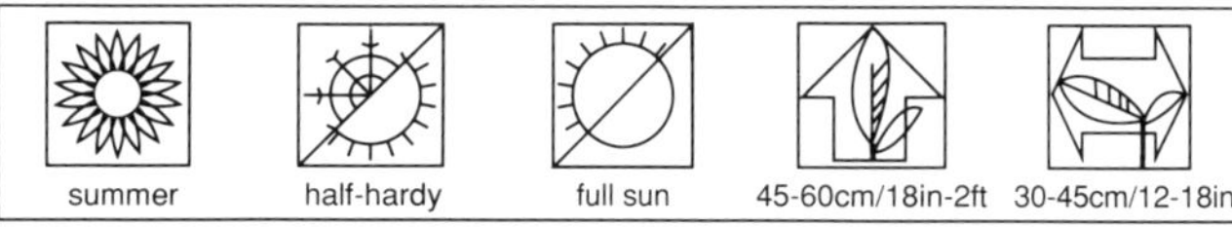

The scented-leaved pot geraniums, more correctly called pelargoniums, have less showy flowers than the zonal, ivy-leaved or regal types, but are an excellent addition to the scented herb garden in summer. There are many to choose from, with leaf scents reminiscent of lemon, pepper, rose, peppermint, pine and balm. As they depend on the leaves being brushed or lightly crushed to release their perfume, and they are tender plants, it is best to grow them in raised beds or pots, where they are accessible and easily moved under cover in winter, if necessary. The small flowers can be eaten in salads and the leaves laid under baked apples to add flavour. They will continue growing indoors as pot plants through winter and make bushy plants when mature.

PROPAGATION Take cuttings of non-flowering shoots (or remove flowers) any time from spring to mid-summer, cutting just below a leaf node. These should root quickly in a well-drained potting medium and can then be potted on.

GROWING Provide winter temperatures of at least 7°C/45°F to keep the plants growing slowly, and keep just moist. Move the plants outside after all danger of frost is past. Water and feed during the growing period.

VARIETIES *Pelargonium graveolens* has a rose scent; *P.* x *fragrans* smells of pine; *P. quercifolium* (*above*) has a spicy perfume.

POSSIBLE PROBLEMS Whitefly.

HELICHRYSUM

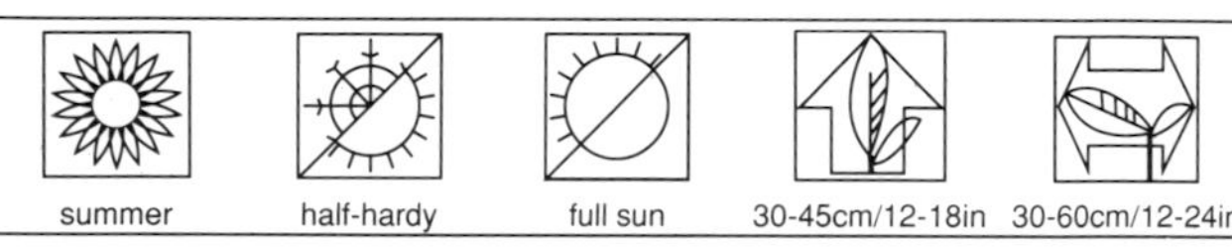

Generally known as the everlasting flower, in fact only the annual helichrysum, *H. bracteatum*, merits the name. The aromatic member of the family is *H. angustifolium (above)*, the curry plant, a bushy, slightly tender perennial with attractive silvery narrow leaves and clusters of small dull-yellow flowers. The whole plant smells of curry, which usually relegates it to the kitchen garden, although the foliage has a bitter taste and cannot be used in cooking. On a warm summer evening the aroma is intense and pervading.

PROPAGATION AND GROWING Plant in well-drained soil in full sun and sheltered from wind. The plant may be badly damaged by frost: better to cut it right back after flowering and protect with straw or leaf mould over winter. To propagate, take cuttings of side shoots in early summer.

VARIETIES There are no named varieties.

POSSIBLE PROBLEMS Generally trouble-free.

HORSERADISH

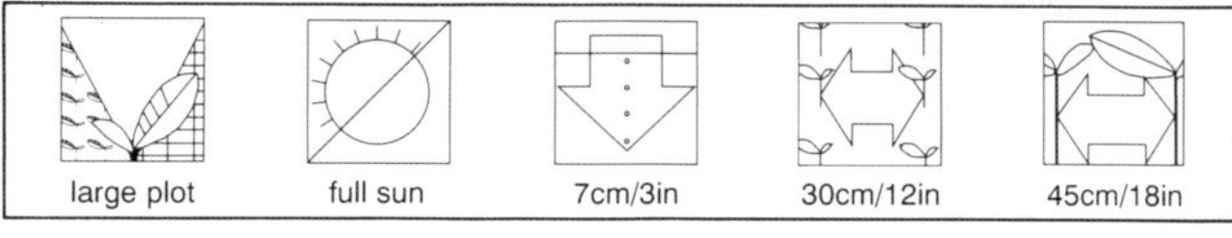

Horseradish is a hardy perennial with large floppy leaves growing from the base of the plant. The flowers are white on a single stem but they do not appear every season. The large thick roots are used sparingly, because of their hot flavour.

GROWING Plant 7-cm/3-in long root cuttings in a rich, moist soil in early spring, 30cm/1ft apart, just covered with soil. An open sunny place is best. These will establish to produce new plants. Lift all the plants in autumn, cut and store the larger roots in sand for winter use, and retain the smaller roots, also in sand, for planting the following spring. This ensures a constant supply of the best quality roots.

HARVESTING Established roots can be dug up as required, but the flavour is improved by cold weather.

POSSIBLE PROBLEMS The roots can become a great invader, so grow horseradish where it can be confined.

USES Horseradish is primarily used as a condiment, grated into cream, and makes a pleasant change from mustard. It is a superb accompaniment to roast or boiled beef. Add grated raw root to coleslaw and uncooked vegetable chutneys. Horseradish sauce helps in the digestion of rich smoked fish, such as eel, mackerel or herring. Horseradish paste made with cream cheese makes a tasty sandwich filling.

HYSSOP

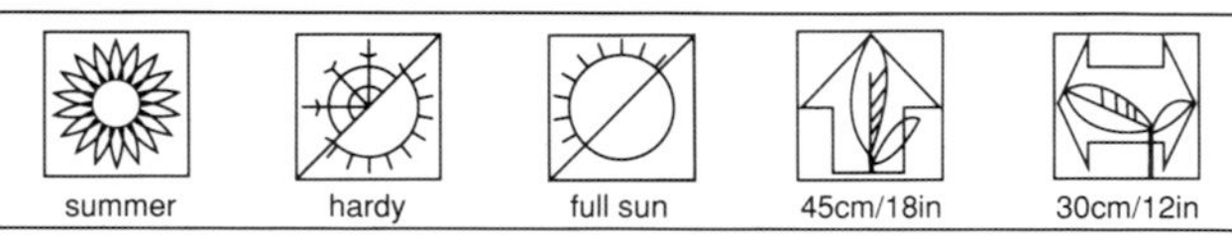

Hyssopus officinalis (above) has been prized as a useful herb for centuries – in the kitchen to preserve meat, as a remedy for coughs and colds and as a strewing herb. It is one of the herbal ingredients of the brandy-based liqueur, Chartreuse, and is also often included in pot-pourris. The small pointed leaves are pleasantly pungent, and the small flowers, which may be blue, pink or white, are sweetly fragrant.

PROPAGATION AND GROWING Hyssop is a decorative plant for the border, for pots, or as a low hedge. Though well-drained soil is preferred, it copes well with moist conditions. Plant from autumn to spring in a sunny position. Dead-head regularly, and cut the whole plant right back in spring. For hedges, set plants 23cm/9in apart and pinch out the growing tips to maintain a bushy shape. Trim lightly in spring. To propagate, raise plants from seed sown in spring, or take basal cuttings, also in spring, to ensure that the coloured varieties do not revert to blue.

VARIETIES As well as the pretty pink and white varieties, *H. o. rosea* and *H. o. alba*, there is a dwarf blue type, ideal for rock gardens, *H. aristatus*.

POSSIBLE PROBLEMS Generally trouble-free.

JUNIPER

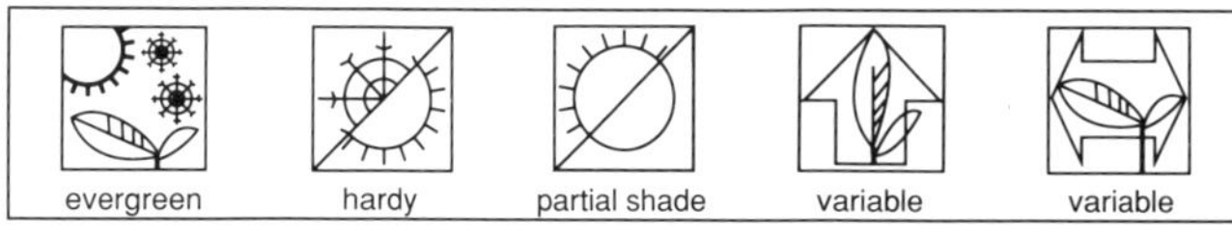

Numerous species of juniper, all evergreen, are cultivated as garden plants. *J. communis* is the one which bears edible berries; 3m/10ft high when mature, its needle-like leaves are grey-green with a white stripe. All parts of the plant are refreshingly aromatic. The berries are picked in their second year, when blue-black and ripe. They are used commercially in the making of gin. For cooking, the berries are first dried. A few crushed berries add distinction to pâtés, stuffings and marinades for game.

PROPAGATION AND GROWING Juniper does well on shallow, chalky soils and in seaside gardens. Set out young plants in late spring, in sun or partial shade. The species may be raised from seed sown in the autumn. Propagate named varieties by cuttings from side shoots taken in autumn.

VARIETIES *J. c.* 'Compressa': one of the smallest at only 45cm/18in after 10 years. Cone-shaped, with silvery leaves, it is ideal for inclusion in a trough of alpines. *J.c.* 'Depressa' *(above)*: low-growing, spreads up to 4m/14ft. *J. c.* 'Depressa Aurea' is a golden-leaved form. Both make excellent ground cover.

POSSIBLE PROBLEMS Scale insects; rust.

LAVENDER

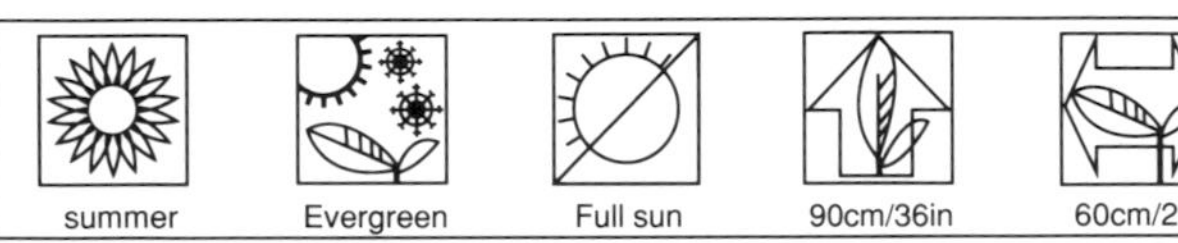

Lavender is a shrubby plant which has been cultivated from ancient times for its refreshing perfume. It has medicinal as well as cosmetic uses. Smoothing lavender oil into the temples is wonderfully relaxing and a sure remedy for tension headaches; massaged into aching muscles (after gardening, perhaps), the oil eases stiffness. Lavender looks superb edging a rose bed or a pathway of brick or old flagstones. The flowers can be dried and used as a base in potpourri.

PROPAGATION AND GROWING Plant between autumn and spring on well-drained soil in full sun. Trim the plants back after flowering to prevent them becoming too leggy. For hedging or alongside a path, set plants 30cm/12in apart and trim in spring. To propagate, take cuttings of non-flowering shoots in late summer. Plants will sometimes self-seed.

VARIETIES *L. spica* or English lavender *(above)*: narrow, silvery leaves, spikes of purple-blue flowers. Recommended varieties include 'Hidcote', sweet scent, violet flowers; 'Folgate', late-flowering, leaves regularly spaced on the stems, blue-mauve flowers; 'Twickel Purple', finest fragrance. *L. stoechas* or French lavender: not fully hardy, overtones of mint to the perfume; large flower-spikes with lasting mauve bracts rise to 60cm/24in from a dense bush of leafy stems.

POSSIBLE PROBLEMS Frost damage; grey mould; honey fungus.

LEMON BALM

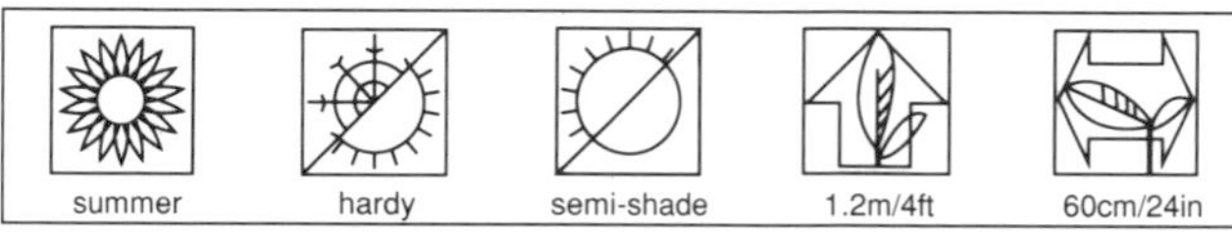

Lemon balm, *Melissa officinalis*, is a bushy herbaceous perennial suitable for mixed borders or to add height at the back of a bed devoted to herbs. It is also known as bee balm, *melissa* being derived from the Greek word for bee. Sprigs of balm are placed in the hive to contain bees when they are restless. The pale green, slightly hairy oval leaves can be used to decorate and add a hint of lemon to summer drinks; the dried leaves are sometimes used in pot pourri. The creamy-white blooms, like nettle flowers, are insignificant.

PROPAGATION AND GROWING Set out young plants in spring or autumn in any ordinary garden soil, in sun or partial shade. Cut stems right back in the autumn and protect the plant from frost in very cold districts. To propagate, divide established plants in the autumn.

VARIETIES 'Aurea' *(above),* known as golden balm, with leaves splashed gold. When cutting back in autumn, leave the stems 15cm/6in long.

POSSIBLE PROBLEMS Generally trouble-free.

LOVAGE

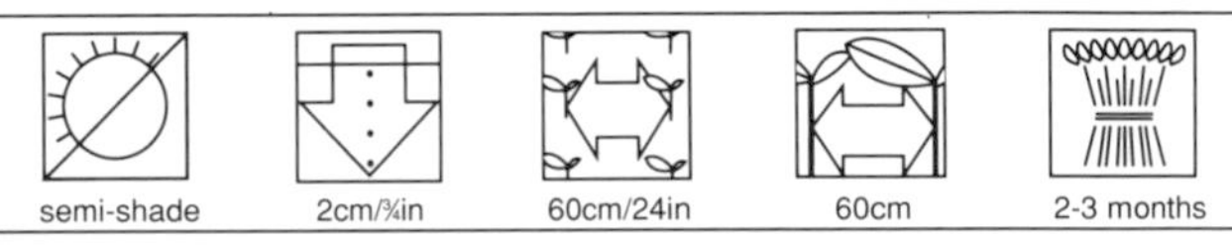

Lovage deserves to be more widely grown by those who have the space. It is a handsome, bushy perennial plant with large but delicate light green leaves. At a possible height of 1.8m/6ft, it is best at the back of the border or providing shelter for smaller specimens. Yellow flowers appear in late summer. The leaves and stems have a celery-like flavour and can be used in any recipe calling for celery. Lovage soup is excellent, and the decorative leaves make a useful garnish. An infusion of the leaves is said to ease kidney ailments and reduce a fever.

PROPAGATION AND GROWING Sow seed in boxes of compost in autumn. Plant out seedlings in moisture-retentive soil the following spring. Leave one or two flowerheads on the plant and it will self seed readily. Alternatively collect seed as soon as it is ripe and treat as above.

VARIETIES There are no varieties of the species, *Levisticum officinale (above)*.

POSSIBLE PROBLEMS Generally trouble-free.

MARIGOLD

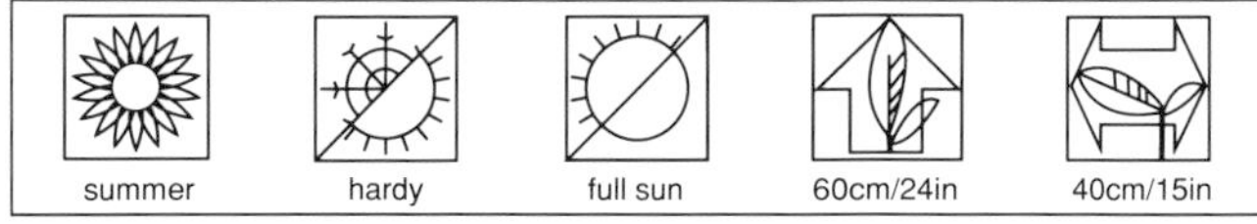

Calendula officinalis (above), is the botanical name for pot marigold, a member of the daisy family with many traditional uses as a culinary and medicinal herb. It is a stalwart of the cottage garden – the roots are said to kill harmful soil bacteria and the smell of the leaves and flowers to discourage whitefly. The vivid orange-yellow petals add colour and pungency to salads; when dried, they can be used to colour savoury rice dishes.

PROPAGATION AND GROWING Marigolds are sturdy annuals that do well in cold climates and in towns. Sow seed in spring in well-drained, good soil, and thin the young plants to 45-60cm/18-24in apart. Remove flowerheads as they fade, leaving one or two on each plant if you want them to self-seed. The bushy habit of growth makes marigolds an ideal container plant.

VARIETIES 'Apricot Beauty'; 'Mandarin'; 'Orange King'.

POSSIBLE PROBLEMS Caterpillars; cucumber mosaic virus; powdery mildew; rust.

MARJORAM

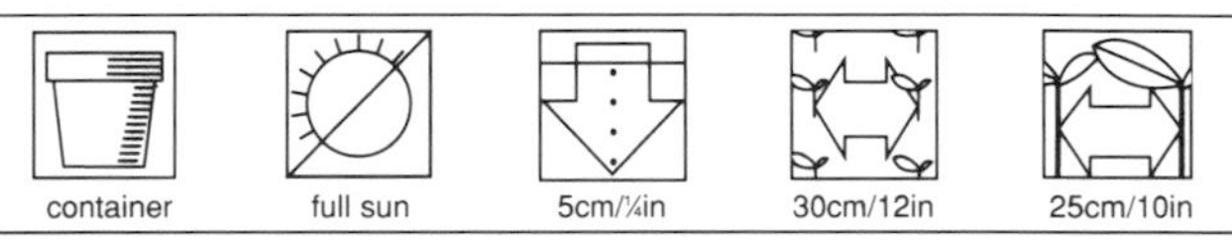

Native to Europe, including Great Britain, marjoram was known to fourteenth-century herbalists, who recommended it in infusions for colds and sore throats. It belongs to the mint family, and the small rounded leaves have an aroma like thyme, but sweeter. Primarily a culinary herb, *Origanum majorana* – sweet marjoram, the best for flavour – is good with meat and stuffings for vegetables. It can also be used in pot-pourri.

PROPAGATION AND GROWING Treat sweet marjoram as a half-hardy annual. Sow seed under protection in early spring. Set out hardened-off plants in early summer in light but fertile soil in a sunny position. Sweet marjoram is useful for edging herb gardens or raised beds of aromatic plants. Perennial species can be increased by cuttings of basal shoots taken in spring.

VARIETIES *O. majorana*, sweet or knotted marjoram: a compact bushy plant 20cm/8in high; *O. onites* or pot marjoram: a hardy perennial with a strong aroma, at 60cm/24in it makes a small shrub for the herb bed; *O. vulgare*, common or wild marjoram, oregano: hardy perennial, up to 45cm/18in high; the decorative variety 'Aureum' *(above)*: has leaves splashed gold.

POSSIBLE PROBLEMS Generally trouble-free.

MINT

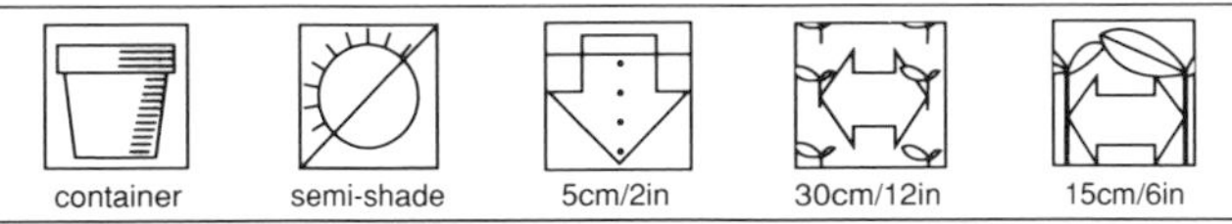

The popularity of the mint family is undeniable; but all the mints are to varying degrees invasive, and will eventually take over the herb bed if left unchecked. Confine mint to tubs or boxes. If you want it in the garden, grow it in a submerged bucket with the bottom knocked out, or restrict the roots with slates buried vertically around them. In English kitchens, mint is traditionally used to make a sauce for roast lamb, or cooked with new potatoes. Mediterranean cooks, recognizing its beneficial effect on the digestion, are more adventurous – mint is used with many vegetables, in yoghurt as a dressing, with fish and salads and with fresh fruit.

PROPAGATION AND GROWING Set out rooted runners of this hardy perennial in spring in rich moist soil. Water well during the growing season and pinch out the tips to encourage a bushy shape. Plants are easy to raise by division in spring.

VARIETIES *Mentha spicata* or common mint, spearmint: 60cm/24in high, pointed leaves; *M. rotundifolia* or apple mint, Bowles' mint *(above)*: round-leaved variety, up to 90cm/3ft high, which is the the cook's favourite. Decorative mints include *M. citrata* or bergamot mint: 30cm/12in high, almost heart-shaped lemony leaves; *M. requienii*: prostrate, spreading, with tiny round peppermint-scented leaves.

POSSIBLE PROBLEMS Rust.

NASTURTIUM

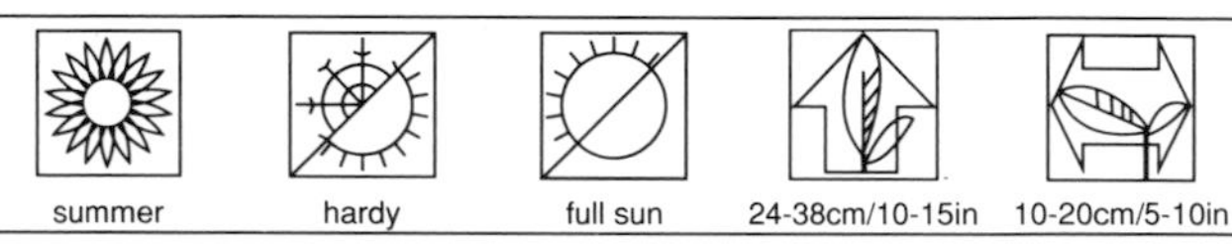

This easily-grown annual herb, properly known as *Tropaeolum majus*, brings a splash of vivid colour to the herb border in summer, with its trumpet-shaped flowers in shades of cream, yellow, orange and scarlet. The flowers are only faintly scented, but the foliage and stalks are richly pungent when crushed. Both flowers and leaves can be eaten fresh in mixed salads and are a good source of vitamin C and iron. Their hot peppery flavour is a little like that of watercress. .

PROPAGATION AND GROWING Large, easily-handled seeds make this an ideal plant for children to sow, and it is unlikely to disappoint. Sow seeds in pots or in the flowering site in mid-spring at a depth of 1cm/¾in. Grown in a sunny, open site in poorish soil, as a rich soil will lead to the production of leaves instead of flowers. Dead-head regularly to prolong flowering. Nasturtiums make excellent edging plants.

VARIETIES There are trailers, climbers and bush forms and a choice of single colours or mixed. 'Tom Thumb' is compact with single flowers in mixed colours; 'Alaska' has variegated leaves and flowers of mixed colours; and 'Whirlybird Scarlet' *(above)* are just a few of the many varieties.

POSSIBLE PROBLEMS Stems and leaves can be heavily infested by the black bean aphid.

PARSLEY

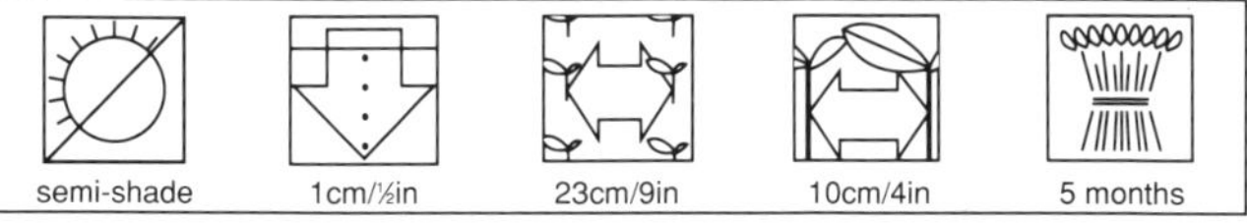

Parsley, *Petroselinum crispum (above)*, belongs to the *Umbelliferae* family, named from the umbel shape of the flower. It is one of the half-dozen most popular herbs and one of the few which good cooks insist on using fresh. It is an essential component of a bouquet garni, and in traditional cottage gardens was often used with alyssum as an edging plant. It attracts bees and is thought to repel greenfly.

PROPAGATION AND GROWING Sow seed outdoors in early spring in moist, rich soil. Parsley is notoriously slow to germinate; delay sowing for a few weeks and the warmer temperature will speed things along. Thin the seedlings to 20cm/8in. Water well in dry weather and cover with cloches if frost threatens. Later sowings, especially in pots that can be brought indoors, will provide leaves well into the winter. Although biennial, parsley is best grown as an annual and raised from fresh seed each year.

VARIETIES Curly-leaved parsley is the variety most often used for garnish, while the French or flat-leaved kind is said to have the better flavour. Plants may be low-growing or reach 60cm/2ft high. Turnip-rooted or Hamburg parsley, *P. c. fusiformis*, is grown for its celery-flavoured roots.

POSSIBLE PROBLEMS Leaf spot; discoloration caused by virus disease.

PENNYROYAL

				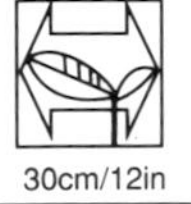
autumn	hardy	semi-shade	7.5cm/3in	30cm/12in

Pennyroyal, *Mentha pulegium (above)*, is a mat-forming species of mint used in fragrant lawns, on paths or as carpet bedding. The aroma of its tiny rounded leaves is piercing rather than sweet and is released when they are crushed underfoot or brushed with the hand. Gardening lore has it that mints make a good growing companion for cabbages – perhaps the strong aroma with which the whole plant is imbued (roots included) keeps pests at bay. It is popularly supposed that the Latin name indicates its efficacy against fleas (for people, not cabbages, that is).

PROPAGATION AND GROWING Set out rooted runners in spring in rich moist soil, about 23cm/9in apart. Divide and replant in spring to propagate.

VARIETIES *M. p. gibraltarica* or Gibraltar mint; a compact variety with dark green, sometimes variegated leaves.

POSSIBLE PROBLEMS Generally trouble-free.

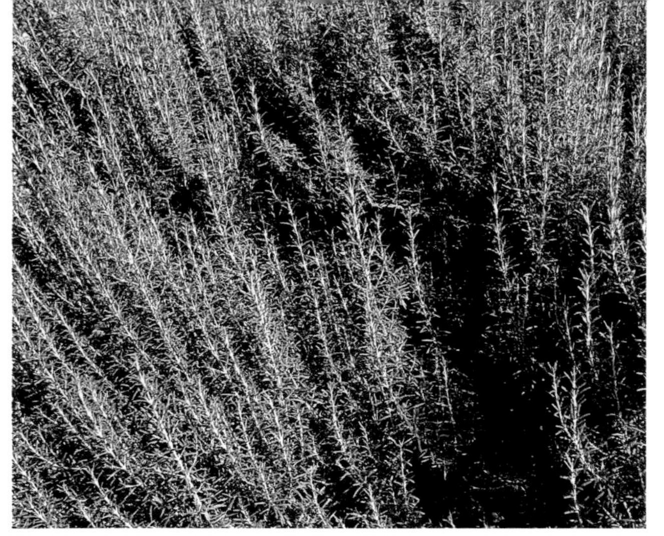

ROSEMARY

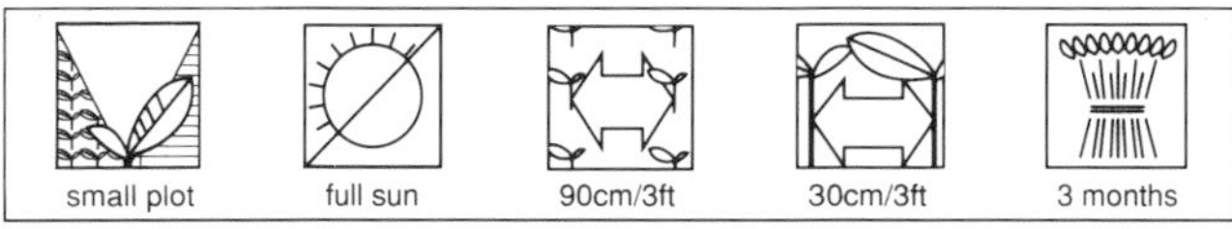

There is an old saying that rosemary will only grow in gardens 'where the mistress is master'. It is to be hoped that in these liberated times gardeners of all persuasions can find a place for it. Hardy almost everywhere, *Rosmarinus officinalis* or common rosemary *(above)*, reaches between 1-2m/3-6ft or more in height, making a dense, semi-erect bush of small, narrow dark green leaves which are intensely aromatic. Pretty pale blue flowers appear in early summer; if you are prepared to forgo them, rosemary can be clipped to make a hedge. The essential oil is an ingredient of eau de Cologne and many other perfumes; in aromatherapy it is used (with lavender) to relieve tension headaches. Because of its powerful aroma, rosemary should be used sparingly when cooking. Elizabeth David recommended basting charcoal-grilled fish with a rosemary branch dipped in olive oil (and finds no other use for it).

PROPAGATION AND GROWING Set young plants in a dry, sunny spot where they can be left to achieve full height. Cut back mature plants to half their height in the autumn to keep the shape neat. Increase by tip cuttings taken in summer.

VARIETIES 'Albiflorus': white flowers; 'Erectus' (syn. 'Fastigiatus'): upright form; 'Humilis': prostrate form spreading to 1.2m/4ft, syn. as *R. lavandulaceus*, not fully hardy.

POSSIBLE PROBLEMS Generally trouble-free.

RUE

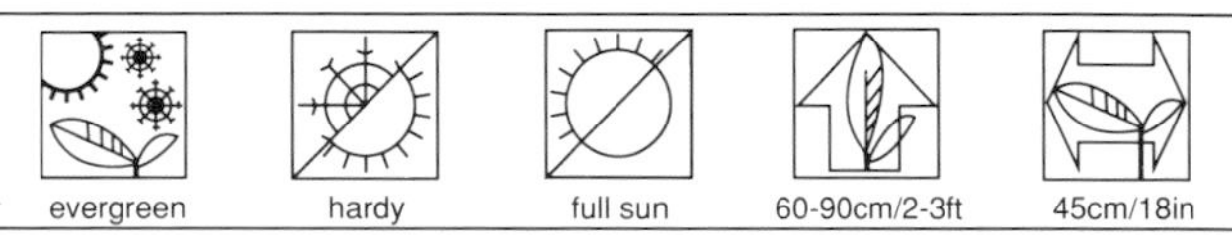

Because of its pungency, rue (*Ruta graveolens*) was included among the strewing herbs used to freshen fifteenth-century households, and in those days was much used in cooking. The flavour is too bitter for modern tastes, however, and it is now grown chiefly for its decorative value. Its blue-green leaves are deeply divided, the whole plant forming a neat rounded shrub. Acid yellow flowers appear in summer. Rue can be planted to form a low hedge, but if the old wives' tale is to be believed, it should not be sited around or near culinary herbs, to which it is supposed to be harmful. Rue looks wonderful in a sunny, mixed border, however, with no ill consequences.

PROPAGATION AND GROWING Plant from autumn to spring in well-drained soil in full sun. Trim back to old wood each spring to prevent the plants becoming leggy. Set plants for hedging 30cm/12in apart and pinch out the growing tips. Propagate by cuttings from side shoots taken in late summer.

VARIETIES 'Jackman's Blue' *(above)*: 45-60cm/18-24in high, suitable for containers, foliage brighter than the species, making a pleasing combination with silver-leaved shrubs.

POSSIBLE PROBLEMS Generally trouble-free.

SAGE

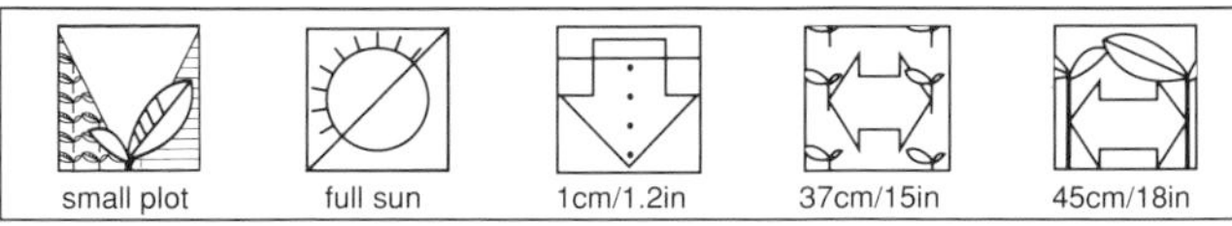

The green-leaved garden sage, *Salvia officinalis (above)*, primarily grown for its culinary uses, has a number of decorative forms, equally useful in the kitchen, which often feature in scented gardens. All are hardy, evergreen sub-shrubs of attractively bushy habit, reaching about 60cm/24in. The slightly bitter oval leaves can be used in any number of dishes, whether based on meat, fish, eggs or vegetables. They retain their flavour well when dried and in combination with onion are traditionally used as a stuffing for roast pork. In Tudor times, an infusion of sage leaves was prescribed for coughs and colds, for constipation, as a mouthwash and a hair conditioner – a versatile herb indeed. It is, after all, related to clary, the ancients' 'cure-all' and still used in perfumery.

PROPAGATION AND GROWING Sow seed in the open in late spring in a sunny position in well-drained soil. Remove flowers as they appear. Trim plants two or three times during the summer; they become leggy after a few years and should be replaced. Propagate from cuttings taken in early autumn.

VARIETIES Purple-leaved and variegated forms are recommended. *S. rutilans* or pineapple sage is a decorative plant bearing tubular scarlet flowers during the summer. The leaves smell of pineapple when crushed but have no culinary uses.

POSSIBLE PROBLEMS Generally trouble-free.

SALAD BURNET

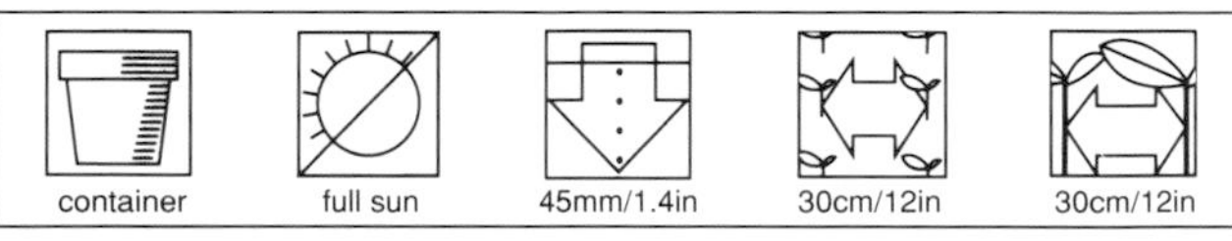

Salad burnet, *Sanguisorba minor (above)*, can be found growing wild on grassland in Great Britain, particularly where the soil is chalky. It is a hardy perennial of the rose family forming a neat clump of foliage with many pairs of deeply toothed leaflets rather like those of a wild rose. The leaves have a pleasant cucumber-like fragrance, making them suitable for salads, as a garnish, or to float in cold drinks. They must be used fresh. Attractive rosy-lilac flowers appear on top of erect stems throughout the summer. Plants are variable in height, from 15-60cm/6-24in.

PROPAGATION AND GROWING Sow seed in late spring on light soil in sun or partial shade. When the flowers appear, pluck them off to encourage leafy growth. Burnet is wind-pollinated and self-seeds easily. It can be propagated by division but the flavour is better in plants raised from seed.

VARIETIES There are no named varieties.

POSSIBLE PROBLEMS Generally trouble-free.

SORREL

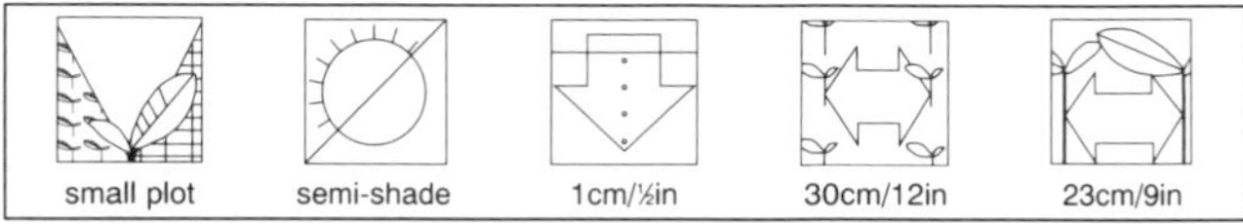

Sorrel is a herbaceous perennial plant, dying down to ground level in autumn. The leaves are fleshy, light green and rather rounded; the tiny pink-red flowers that appear in early to mid summer should be removed.

GROWING A moist, fertile soil, such as a well-broken-down clay, gives good leaf size and succulence. Put in young plants in spring or autumn, 23cm/9in apart. Sun is preferred but sorrel will grow in shade.

HARVESTING Cut one or two leaves from each plant when individual plants have formed a group of more than five leaves, usually about three months after plants start to grow. Continue to harvest as required until the plants die back in autumn.

POSSIBLE PROBLEMS Soup recipes recommend 450g/1lb of leaves at a time, so a large harvest is needed. Whether you include this unusual herb in the kitchen garden depends upon how much space you want to devote to its cultivation.

USES Sorrel makes the famous and delicious sorrel soup, so popular in France, with a pleasantly sour flavour. It goes well with salads, and other vegetables, if used in moderation.

SUMMER PURSLANE

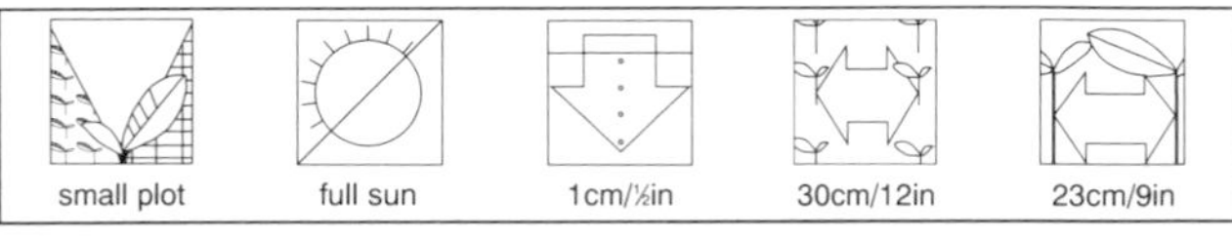

Summer purslane is not a commonly grown leaf vegetable. It is worth trying if only because it grows very quickly. A low-growing plant, it can be cooked or eaten raw in salads.

GROWING Sandy soil suits summer purslane best, and a warm and sheltered position. Mixing the fine seed beforehand with moist sand will make sowing easier. Sow the seed broadcast from late spring until late summer. The plant usually grows well under the protection of glass or plastic cloches, but during wet, cold summers it often fails in the open.

HARVESTING Summer purslane is ready for picking in about 6 weeks – it may be ready in as little as 4 weeks, if the weather is warm or if it is grown under cloches. A length of stalk is usually picked with the leaves.

POSSIBLE PROBLEMS Over-close planting and over-watering can result in the fungus disease smoulder.

SUMMER SAVORY

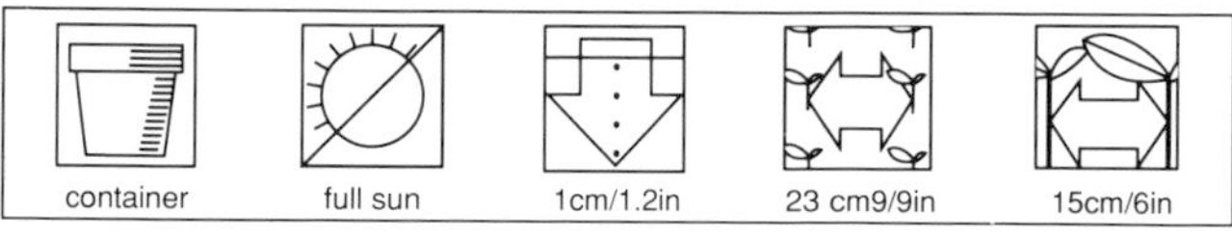

The ancient Romans used the leaves of *Satureia hortensis* or summer savory *(above)*, to make a popular flavoured vinegar, and they believed the fragrance of the plant to be particularly attractive to bees. Since the leaves are soothing to insect bites, perhaps it is just as well the plants were often sited near the hives. The dark green leaves of this hardy annual are narrow and tapering, the plant bushy and upright to about 30cm/12in. Pale lilac flowers appear from the leaf axils throughout the summer. Savory is said to be a good growing partner for broad beans, acting as a repellent to blackfly. It is certainly a good companion to the beans once cooked, indeed with many bean dishes. The slightly spicy flavour gives it a place in bouquets garnis too, or boiled with new potatoes instead of mint.

PROPAGATION AND GROWING Sow seed in spring in fertile, well-drained soil in shallow drills, and thin to their final spacings when large enough to handle. For a winter supply, sow seeds in pots in late summer and keep at a minimum temperature of 7°C/45°F.

VARIETIES *S. montana* or winter savory; a perennial, almost evergreen sub-shrub, 30cm/12in high, grey-green foliage of inferior flavour.

POSSIBLE PROBLEMS Generally trouble-free.

SWEET CICELY

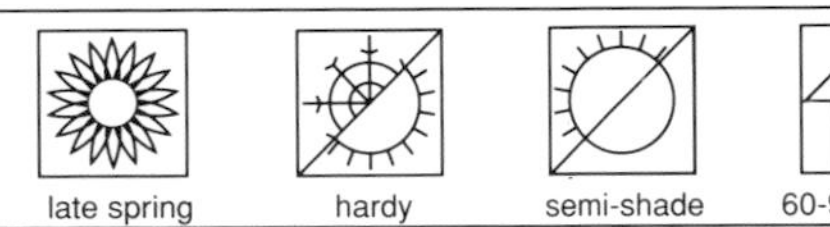

A herbaceous perennial, sweet cicely, *Myrrhis odorata (above)*, belongs to the family *Umbelliferae*, in company with parsley, coriander, dill and a long list of plants both decorative and edible. Since it may reach 1.5m/5ft in favourable conditions, sweet cicely is best situated at the back of the border or herb bed, carrying its white flowers aloft. A pleasant scent reminiscent of aniseed is emitted by the large, fern-like leaves which, like the hollow stems, are covered in soft hairs. As the plant ages, the stems redden and the flowers give way to long, black seeds. Use the leaves when stewing tart fruits as a sweetener, or add them to fresh fruit salads. Chew the seeds to relieve indigestion.

PROPAGATION AND GROWING Sow seed in early spring in any ordinary garden soil. Choose a sheltered spot in sun or semi-shade: sweet cicely is a good candidate for the wild garden as it self-seeds readily. Alternatively plants may be divided in the autumn. If you do not want the seeds and wish to contain the spread of the plant, remove the flowers as soon as they fade.

VARIETIES There are no named varieties.

POSSIBLE PROBLEMS Generally trouble-free.

SWEET WOODRUFF

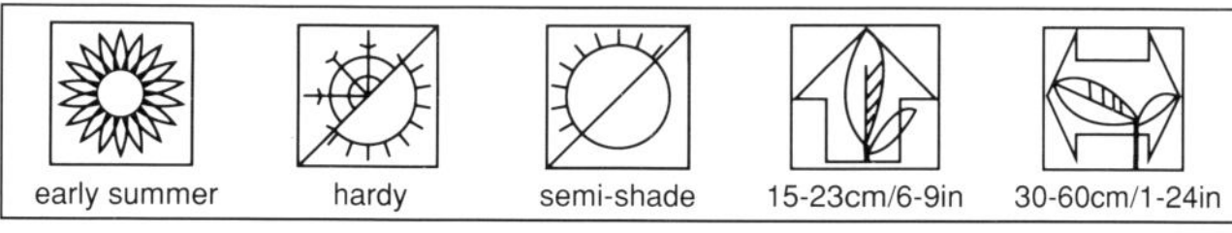

Galium odoratum syn. *Asperula odorata (above)*, was one of the herbs used in Tudor times for 'strewing'. When dried it smells of new-mown hay, and was mixed with dried mint, thyme, hyssop and chamomile and cast on the floor to release their fragrance when walked upon (and, more practically, to inhibit household vermin). Woodruff belongs to a huge and varied family of plants which includes two famous for their aroma – gardenias and coffee. This less exotic species has shiny green lanceolate leaves and bears clusters of small white flowers in early summer. Woodruff grows wild in British woodland; in the garden it is useful as ground cover.

PROPAGATION AND GROWING Set out plants in groups from autumn to spring, in moist soil. Woodruff will do well under trees. To propagate, simply divide and replant at any time from autumn to spring.

VARIETIES There are no named varieties.

POSSIBLE PROBLEMS Generally trouble-free.

TANSY

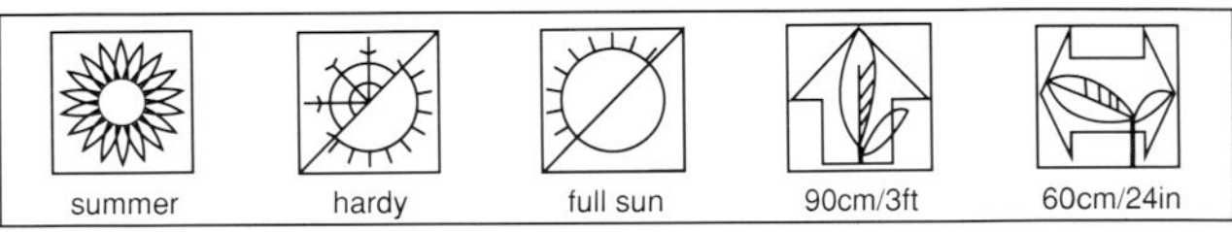

This old cottage garden favourite – *Tanacetum vulgare (above)*, commonly known as buttons – is a member of the daisy family which bears flat clusters of small, yellow flowers at the top of long straight stems. A camphor-like fragrance resides in the large, deeply cut leaves, which have been used in many ways down the centuries, primarily as a tonic when infused in hot water. Tansy cakes used to be made at Easter, the slightly bitter leaves adding spice and bite to the mixture.

PROPAGATION AND GROWING A strong growing perennial, tansy can become a nuisance in the garden if left unchecked. Plant in any well-drained soil in spring or autumn. Remove flowerheads as they fade. Propagate by division in spring.

VARIETIES There are no named varieties, and alpine species of *Tanacetum* are not aromatic.

POSSIBLE PROBLEMS Generally trouble-free.

TARRAGON

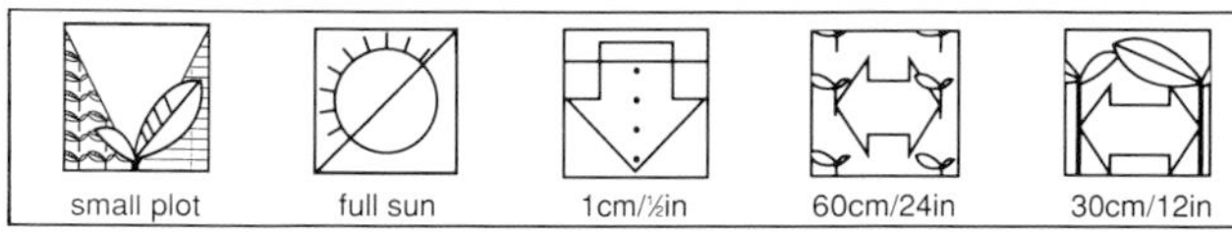

Tarragon is a culinary herb of the genus *Artemisia*. There are two species for the kitchen garden: *A. dranunculus (above)* or French tarragon is far superior to Russian tarragon, *A. dranunculoides*, which is somewhat lacking in aroma; 'dranunculus', on the other hand, means 'dragon-like', which might as well refer to the sharp pointed leaves as to their incomparable flavour.

PROPAGATION AND GROWING Set out groups of young plants in good, well-drained soil in spring or autumn. Full sun is essential, and it is advisable to feed the plants during the growing season to achieve a good flavour. Pinch out the growing tips to encourage leaf development. As tarragon is a perennial: cut down the plants in late autumn and cover with straw to protect from frost. Divide and replant every 3 years in fresh soil, or treat as annuals.

VARIETIES *A. dranunculoides* lacks the sharp aniseed flavour of *A. dranunculus.*

POSSIBLE PROBLEMS Generally trouble-free.

THYME

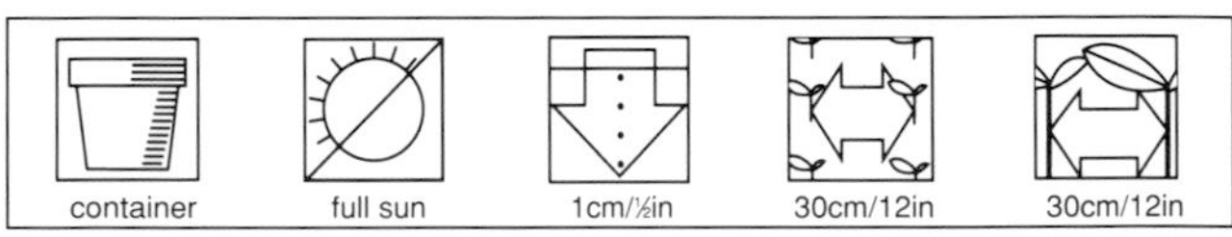

In any argument about the queen of herbs, you can count on a majority in favour of thyme. Maybe this is because there are so many that everyone can find a species of this evergreen shrub exactly to their taste. Once used as a strewing herb, and with medicinal applications ranging from a poultice for boils to a tonic bath or an ointment for insect bites, today thyme predominates in the kitchen. It is included in bouquets garnis, in stuffings, with vegetables, in omelettes and on pizzas. Place a sprig underneath a roasting joint or fowl. Dried thyme keeps its flavour well.

PROPAGATION AND GROWING Plant in spring in a sunny position in well-drained soil. Thyme is excellent in troughs, as an edging plant and for ground cover. Replace the plants when they become leggy. Propagate by division in spring.

VARIETIES *Thymus vulgaris* or common thyme *(above)*: height up to 20cm/8in, dark green narrow leaves, good flavour. *T.v.* 'Aureus' is an ornamental golden-leaved form. *T.* × *citriodorus* or lemon-scented thyme: height up to 30cm/12in, broader leaves; silver and gold-leaved forms are available. *T. herba-barona* or caraway thyme: mat-forming species, not fully hardy, traditionally used to flavour roast beef.

POSSIBLE PROBLEMS Generally trouble-free.

WINTER PURSLANE

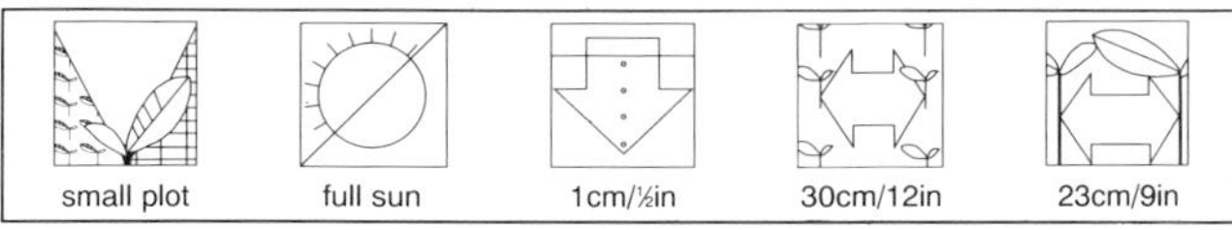

Late-sown crops of winter purslane survive mild winters and form a useful ingredient in the vegetable garden in early spring. Winter purslane is a low-growing, succulent salad plant.

GROWING Sow the seed from early spring to late summer in its final position. Most ordinary soils will be suitable and the plants tolerate light shade. Thin the seedlings to 10-13cm/4-5in apart each way.

HARVESTING The young leaves are ready for picking from 30 days.

POSSIBLE PROBLEMS Over-close planting and over-watering can result in the fungus disease smoulder. Protect winter purslane from frost by covering with cloches.

Pests & Diseases

PESTS

PROBLEM	DAMAGE CAUSED	REMEDY
Aphids (greenfly, blackfly)	Sap sucked; honeydew emitted; virus diseases spread	Spray with pirimicarb
Capsid bug	Leaves tattered or with tiny holes	Spray with systemic insecticide
Caterpillar	Leaves, stems, flowers eaten	Spray with permethrin
Eelworm	Plants weakened; leaves and stems distorted	Destroy infected plants; do not grow again on same site
Froghopper	Sap sucked under cuckoospit	Spray with fenitrothion
Mealy bug	Sap sucked; virus diseases spread by small insect enclosed in white 'wool'	Spray with malathion
Narcissus fly	No flowers; weak, grassy leaves; maggots in bulbs	Destroy infested (soft) bulbs
Red-spider mite	Sap sucked; foliage desiccated; fine webs spun	Spray with fenitrothion or malathion
Scale insects	Sap sucked; virus diseases spread by small, limpet-like insects	Spray with malathion
Slugs and snails	Young plant leaves eaten	Scatter methiocarb thinly among plants
Thrips	White speckles, then grey patches on leaves, flowers	Spray with fenitrothion
Vine weevil	Lower leaves holed and notched; grubs on roots; plants wilt	Dust lower leaves and soil with HCH
Whitefly	Sap sucked; virus diseases spread	Spray with permethrin

DISEASES

PROBLEM	DAMAGE CAUSED	REMEDY
Bacterial canker	Leaves full of holes; stem cankers with oozing gum; general weakening	Cut out infected wood; spray with benomyl
Botrytis (grey mould)	Parts of plants rot, become covered in grey fur	Remove and burn infected parts; spray with benomyl
Canker	Rough brown sunken areas on stems	Cut out and burn; spray with thiophanate-methyl
Chlorosis	Leaves yellowed; growth stunted on alkaline soils	Grow plants on acid soils; water with iron sequestrene; feed well
Die-back	Woody stems die at tip	Cut out infected wood back to healthy tissue
Fusarium wilt	Lower leaves and stem bases turn brown and rot	Destroy infected plants; do not grow species again on same ground
Root rot	Roots turn brown and rot killing plant	Destroy infected plants
Rust	Yellow spots on upper leaf surfaces, orange pustules below	Destroy infected plants; spray others with mancozeb; prevent by growing resistant strains
Virus diseases	Leaves distorted, marbled, yellowed; plant often stunted	Dig up and burn; control insect disease carriers

Glossary

Acid Used to describe soil with a pH reading below 7.0. Because acid soil contains little lime, lime-hating plants like rhododendrons thrive in them.

Alkaline Used to describe soil with a pH reading above 7.0. A slightly alkaline soil suits most plants.

Annual A plant that completes its life cycle in one growing season.

Biennial A plant that needs two growing seasons to complete its life cycle.

Bract A modified leaf, which may be coloured and have the appearance of a petal.

Cloche Glass or plastic covering to protect plants in the open.

Compost 1 a mixture of loam, sand, peat and leaf-mould used for growing plants in containers. 2 rotted remains of plant and other organic material.

Crown The bottom of a perennial such as lupin from which roots and shoots arise.

Dormant Literally, sleeping. Used to describe the period when a plant makes no growth, usually in the winter.

Fungicide A substance used to combat fungal diseases.

Germination The first stage in the development of a plant from a seed.

Half-hardy Used to describe plants that require protection during the winter.

Hardy Description of plants that survive frost in the open.

Humus The substance remaining when dead vegetable matter has broken down.

Insecticide A substance used for killing insects.

Neutral Used to describe soil with a pH reading between 6.5 and 7.0, which is neither acid nor alkaline.

Peat Partially decayed organic matter. Sedge peat is from the roots of sedges growing in bogs.

Perennial A plant that lives for an indefinite period.

pH reading The pH scale is used to measure the acidity or alkalinity of soil. The neutral point is 7.0; a reading above this denotes alkalinity and one below it denotes acidity.

Pinching out Removing the growing point of a stem to encourage bushy growth.

Pricking out Planting out seedlings for the first time to larger trays or to a nursery bed.

Propagation Increasing plants.

Seedling A young plant.

Stamen The male reproductive organ of a flower arising from the centre of the petals.

Tender Used to describe any plant susceptible to damage by frost.

Tilth The surface layer of the soil, which is fine and crumbly.

Transplanting Moving young plants from one place to another to give them more room to develop.

Index